They Think It's All Over ...

They Think It's All Over ...

Memories of the Greatest Day in English Football

Kenneth Wolstenholme

Robson Books

First published in Great Britain in 1996 by Robson Books Ltd, Bolsover House, 5–6 Clipstone Street, London W1P 8LE

British Library Cataloguing in Publication Data
A catalogue record for this title is available from the British Library

ISBN 1 86105 022 4

Set in Palatino by Columns Design Ltd of Reading
Printed in Great Britain by Butler & Tanner Ltd,
Frome and London.

Contents

Foreword
by Ian Wooldridge

Kenneth Wolstenholme should never have been a football commentator. Confronted by odds that make Russian roulette seem comparatively safe, he should have been dead. A curious way, you may say, to introduce a book by a man you admire and claim to be a friend, but hear me out. Between 1942 and the end of World War Two the young Wolstenholme flew exactly 100 missions with the RAF over Germany, first in daylight bombers and then, even more precariously, with Donald Bennett's celebrated Pathfinder Force which struck first by dropping marker flares on to the target. The death toll was appalling. Some never survived their first raid, 25 missions suggested that Someone Up There was in your team, 50 were regarded as breaking point. Ken achieved 100 and won the Distinguished Flying Cross and Bar.

When he started commentating on football for the BBC in 1947 that wartime experience dictated his approach. He could see sport in its true perspective. Football was not a matter of life and death, as Bill Shankly was so absurdly to proclaim. And so, when the likes of Hidegkúti, Puskas and Kocsis came to Wembley in 1953 and ran rings round England, it might have been the end of England's supremacy in Europe but it wasn't the end of the world. Ken sustained that attitude until he left the BBC in 1971.

As a commentator he was gifted in three ways: a good knowledge of the game, a beautiful speaking voice and a respect for the English language. During his era, with Peter O'Sulleven calling the horses, Dan Maskell reporting from Wimbledon and the incomparable Henry Longhurst covering Open Golf Championships with long silences broken by penetrating shafts of wit and wisdom, Britain enjoyed a golden age of television sports commentating.

Kenneth Wolstenholme covered more than 2,000 matches for the BBC before moving on. On the afternoon of 30 July 1966, he ad-libbed five words into a microphone at Wembley that were destined to be re-broadcast more times than Winston Churchill's 'We shall fight on the beaches' exhortation.

'They think it's all over', he said as spectators swarmed on to the pitch convinced England had beaten Germany 3–2 to win the World Cup. Then, as Geoff Hurst added England's fourth, he calmly added: 'It is now.'

Wolstenholme didn't much bother about players' birthdays, their wives' names or whether they had some aunt who had once played in *Coronation Street*. He criticized but didn't denigrate and I never once heard him patronize. I guess it is something you learn over places like Dortmünd and Berlin at dead of night.

Introduction

Thirty years is a long time, but it is not long enough to wipe out the memories of perhaps the greatest day in England's sporting history, the day England won THE World Cup. I use capital letters for the definite article because I cannot think of any other genuine World Cup. Rugby Union's comes the closest, but the number of competing nations is puny compared with the number taking part in the football version. The cricket World Cup can be discounted as a Mickey Mouse tournament insofar as it is a competition of one-day cricket with all sorts of artificial rules.

But the World Cup England won on 30 July 1966 was a truly major competition with the seventy participating countries being whittled down to sixteen before the final stages.

World Cups, World Championships, Olympic Games and other big sporting occasions are more often remembered for their arguments and ill feeling than for any cementing of friendships, but the 1966 World Cup, though it had the odd hiccup, was generally played in true sporting spirit. The Final itself was a real carnival, with not a single trace of animosity, despite two disputed goals, and despite the absence of both segregation or fencing in of spectators.

Most people who were there have happy memories of it. The story of Ken Ashman, from Waterlooville, is typical:

I travelled extensively in pursuance of the means of 'earning a crust', very often visiting Germany. One of my German colleagues was one of four who played bridge every week, with all winnings being put into a kitty and blown once a year.

In 1966 they decided it would be a good idea to go to the World Cup Final at Wembley, although they didn't know at the time which teams would be in the Final. I was asked to get the tickets. To do that, it was necessary to buy sets of tickets covering all the matches being played at Wembley. I applied for and obtained five sets of tickets, thereby enabling myself, together with members of my family and friends, to attend all the England matches at Wembley.

The day of the Final arrived. The four Germans and myself were surrounded by English fans. When the disputed goal [England's third] was being referred to the Russian linesman, one of my German friends said to me, 'He will give a goal. He is a communist.'

When the final whistle was blown, a cockney, who had been standing behind us, said to me very, very slowly and very deliberately, 'We ... think ... you ... played ... very ... well.'

Not wishing to cause any embarrassment, I replied, '*Dankeschön,*' one of the few German phrases in my vocabulary.

It's true that some fans went onto the pitch in the last seconds, but there was no malice in their action, as one of them, Michael Richardson, explains:

I was just seventeen and had got my first job playing the drums in a band at Tiffany's in Piccadilly Circus. Our keyboard player had a ticket for the Final but didn't want to go, so I gave him a fiver for it.

England were 3–2 up when I saw the referee put his whistle in his mouth. I thought he was going to blow for the end of the match and I was so elated, so carried away that England had won that I climbed over the small concrete wall with about five other people. I don't think any of us got more than one pace inside the playing pitch. Certainly we didn't interfere with the play. We just wanted to congratulate the English players.

I saw Geoff Hurst shoot, but I didn't see the ball go into the net because I was grabbed by about half a dozen policemen. They were quite friendly and one of them said, 'Now we don't want anyone being naughty and running onto the pitch.'

With that they gently lowered me back into the crowd.

It was Rogan Taylor, Director of the Football Research Unit at Liverpool University and consultant on that splendid television programme, *Kicking and Screaming*, who first suggested that I revive my memories of the tournament at which I was privileged to be the number one commentator for BBC Television.

The 1966 World Cup was the highlight of my career as a commentator. A splendidly organized tournament with the breathtaking climax of England winning in extra-time with a disputed goal and then the unforgettable fourth goal by Geoff Hurst thrown in. What could beat that?

By 1971, when the BBC and I parted company after nearly twenty-four years, it was a sad parting engineered by a faction within the Corporation. But what it could not do and will never do, is diminish the happy memories I have of being the commentator on the greatest day of English football.

So I must thank Rogan Taylor for persuading me to write my story. I approached Robson Books, received wonderful encouragement from them, and this book is the result.

Writing the book has been a labour of love, but my thanks are due to many people besides Rogan and the staff of Robson Books. Jan Sewell read every draft, made suggestions and corrections and gave encouragement. Without that help the book would never have been finished.

Most of all, my thanks are due to Sir Alf Ramsey and the squad he selected. It was they who won the World Cup, and if they hadn't there would have been no book. Not only did they win the World Cup, but all of them have cooperated magnificently in answering all my questions. Those who were not in the team selected to play in the Final have been just as helpful as those who were. The video firm of C-21-C were most generous in allowing me to use their interview with Antonio Rattin.

There are five people I would have liked to talk with but regretfully couldn't. George Eastham and Terry Paine now live in South Africa. Sadly, both the physios – Harold Shepherdson and Les Cocker – have died. So, too, has the man who captained England to her greatest footballing triumph – Bobby Moore.

What can anyone add to the many tributes which have been paid to Bobby, or Mooro as the fans loved to call him?

In May 1995 the first Bobby Moore Fund Golf Day was held at Mannings Heath Golf Club. Terry Venables wrote this in the programme:

A numbing sense of incredible loss enveloped us all when the great Bobby Moore died on 24 February 1993.

For Bobby Moore was indeed a colossus. A giant of a man. Steadfastly loyal, genuinely warm, and the most generous of social companions.

I shall never forget the sight of Bobby Moore receiving what was then the Jules Rimet Trophy from Her Majesty The Queen (after he had wiped his hands clean on the seat of his shorts!), then turning round and holding the trophy aloft. Nor shall I forget my words on the commentary, 'It is only twelve inches high, it's solid gold and it means England are the World Champions.'

Nor shall I ever forget being in a packed Westminster Abbey at Bobby's Memorial Service and hearing that part of my commentary replayed. I was proud to think that was my personal tribute to a great man.

This book is dedicated to the memory of men like Bobby Moore, Les Cocker and Harold Shepherdson, and to those who are happily still with us, Sir Alf Ramsey and his World Cup winning squad.

They were THE MEN OF 1966.

1

Alf Ramsey Takes Charge

World Cup Final: England 4 – West Germany 2 (after extra-time).

That was the score flash which sent everyone in England wild with delight just before half-past five on the afternoon of Saturday, 30 July 1966. It meant that England, universally accepted as the home of football – except by the Scots, of course – were the World Champions. It was a scoreline which triggered off celebrations the like of which hadn't been seen since those heady days of VE and VJ day.

The players became immediate heroes. Some of them were later to appear in the Honours List. For Alf Ramsey there was a Knighthood. It was a well-deserved and popular honour for the man who had masterminded the greatest moment in the history of English football. But it had not been a smooth ride to glory.

Alf Ramsey had taken over the England managership from Walter (now Sir Walter) Winterbottom in January 1963. Unlike Winterbottom he was not encumbered by a Selection Committee from the Football Association whose qualifications for picking an international side were vividly described in a chapter of Len Shackleton's autobiography. In the chapter entitled 'What Directors Know About Football', Len left a blank page! Instead of a Selection Committee Alf had an International Committee, whose members went to the games and to the receptions but had no say in the selection of the team. That was Alf Ramsey's job. He was exposed to the praise and to the criticism – and there was to be more of the latter than of the former.

Alf Ramsey soon found out that he had a job on his hands. His first task was to try to ensure England's survival in the European Championship (then called the European Nations Cup) in a tie against France at the Parc des Princes in Paris on 27 February 1963. In the first leg at Hillsborough, England had given a shocking performance and just managed to scrape a 1–1 draw, but the public were certain that Alf Ramsey could wave the magic wand in Paris and beat France, who had a dismal record of not having won a match for eighteen months.

It is interesting to note the team Alf chose: Ron Springett (Sheffield Wednesday); Jimmy Armfield (Blackpool), captain, Brian Labone (Everton), Bobby Moore (West Ham United), Ron Henry (Tottenham Hotspur); John Connelly (Burnley), Bobby Charlton (Manchester United), Ron Flowers (Wolves), Bobby Tambling (Chelsea); Jimmy Greaves (Tottenham Hotspur), Bobby Smith (Tottenham Hotspur).

Sadly, the magic wand didn't work. France were a goal up in three minutes, 3–0 up at half-time and, although Greaves and Tambling both scored to give England a flicker of a chance, a couple more late French goals turned a sad English performance into a rout.

The sports writers started sharpening their knives. Would they begin to use them before Alf had time to sort the wheat from the chaff and work out a winning formula? And how patient would the fans be?

All this must seem only too familiar to those managers through the years whose task has been no different from Alf Ramsey's – trying to build a team to do well in international competition.

Alf Ramsey faced a painful three years in which to find a squad capable of winning the World Cup, yet he could only feed his hopes on a diet of non-competition matches. Arranging even friendlies was going to be difficult enough because other countries would not want to give him too many clues, so would steer clear of a fixture against England whenever possible.

It would be easy to chop and change the side and give as many players as possible a chance to show what they could do. But Alf didn't like chopping and changing and believed that any player selected for England deserved to be given enough time to prove his worth.

In those days the England manager was not, unlike what happens now, given the luxury of a free Saturday for the First Division teams before a mid-week international, and it was surprising how many players were reported by their clubs as unfit, for various reasons, to turn out for England on a Wednesday, only to make a recovery remarkable enough to enable them to be pronounced fit to play in a league game the following Saturday.

The rebuilding work that Alf Ramsey did on the England team shows in the fact that only two of the players who were in the side beaten by France in Paris in 1963 survived to play in the 1966 Final of the World Cup. They were Bobby Moore and Bobby Charlton.

The immediate fixture list looked daunting. Some six weeks after the débâcle in France there was a match against Scotland at Wembley and that would be followed by a visit from Brazil, the reigning World Champions. The close-season tour included two matches in Eastern Europe – against Czechoslovakia in Bratislava and East Germany in Leipzig – and a final match against Switzerland in Basle.

Still smarting at the exit from the European Championships, Ramsey dropped five players from the side which had lost to France for the game against Scotland at Wembley on 6 April. Out went Ron Springett, Ron Henry, Brian Labone, John Connelly and Bobby Tambling. In came Maurice Norman, of Spurs, and Bryan Douglas, of Blackburn Rovers. Gordon Banks (then with Leicester City) and the Liverpool pair of Gerry Byrne and Jimmy Melia, were called up to make their international débuts.

The changes didn't bring victory. Scotland, as so often in the run-up to the World Cup finals (not to mention just after the 1966 victory!) were England's bogey team. They won 2–1.

Two straight defeats for England. Not a happy omen for the new manager, nor much encouragement for the visit of the reigning World Champions a month later. . . .

Ramsey decided on three more changes: Ray Wilson, of Huddersfield Town, replaced Gerry Byrne, Gordon Milne (Liverpool) made his début at the expense of Ron Flowers, and George Eastham, of Arsenal, also came in for his first cap to the exclusion of Melia.

The selection of Eastham, which must have brought great joy to the Eastham family because his father, also called George, had been capped for England in 1935, when a Bolton Wanderers player, also came as a great surprise.

Many people believed Eastham had been blacklisted after his successful court action in 1963 which effectively ended the retain-and-transfer system. Perhaps he would have been in the old days when the international side was selected by a

Football Association committee, but Alf Ramsey was obviously only concerned with footballing ability.

George Eastham will always be remembered as the man who opened the door for the revolution in the players' terms and conditions of employment. He was, in fact, a forerunner of Marc Bosman, the Belgian footballer who in 1995 threw the game into upheaval by winning the same rights of employment for footballers as those enjoyed by other citizens. I wonder, though, whether there would ever have been a Bosman if there hadn't been an Eastham.

Brazil came to England in the middle of a European tour. They had beaten West Germany 2–1 in Hamburg three days before the Wembley game but that had been only their second victory in the five matches so far on the tour. Not only that, Brazil had been second best for much of the game, and only two brilliant goals inside two minutes had done the trick for them. Coutinho scored the first twenty minutes from the end and then Pelé won the match with a stunning volley from all of thirty yards. (The referee in Hamburg was none other than Mr Dienst, of Switzerland, whom we were to get to know rather better three years later when he refereed the World Cup final.)

Ninety-two thousand people crowded into Wembley Stadium, but there was an early disappointment for them: neither Zito nor Pelé played. They were both recovering from injuries sustained in a taxicab crash in Hamburg forty-eight hours previously. So the game lost a lot of its glamour. Nevertheless, Brazil paraded such stars as Gylmar, Eduardo and Amarildo, so there was enough talent to worry the England side.

On paper, a 1–1 draw against Brazil could be rated an excellent performance by England, but without Pelé and their captain, Zito, Brazil showed little appetite for attacking football, strangely enough for them. My memory of the game is mainly of a magnificent display by Bobby Moore, who always seemed to reserve his best form for games against Brazil, thank goodness!

After two defeats, a draw against Brazil put England in good heart for the trip eastwards, as they set off for Bratislava. Meanwhile, Brazil fell into the depths of despair at the San Siro Stadium in Milan where I saw them suffer a shattering 3–0 defeat. Perhaps the poor results of their 1963 European tour were the first sign that the Brazil of 1966 would be nothing like as formidable as the Brazil of 1962, World Cup winners in Chile.

Few people at home realized what a tour in Eastern Europe meant in 1963. Apart from the fact that the Eastern European countries were capable of putting up fierce opposition, both the food and the general living conditions in that part of the world were far from ideal in the 1960s.

So it was never easy to win on these tours, and Czechoslovakia especially were expected to give us a hard time in Bratislava on 20 May. Only twelve months before we met them they had been runners-up in the 1962 World Cup in Chile, scoring first but eventually going down to Brazil. And in their line-up against England they had Schroiff in goal, two superb defenders in Novak and Popluhar and the classy Pluskal and Masopust in midfield.

England made just two changes from the side which had held Brazil: Chelsea's Ken Shellito got his one and only cap at right back and Terry Paine, of Southampton, made his début at outside right.

It was fourth time lucky for Alf Ramsey. After two defeats and a draw his team played superbly against a side which proved full of good football.

Czechoslovakia started brightly enough and stretched the English defence so much that we were thankful for the goal-keeping of Gordon Banks and the superb work of Bobby Moore, who marshalled his troops magnificently. But gradually England got a grip on the game and their football began to match their spirit. They were two up at half-time, thanks to a typically cheeky goal by Greaves and a beautiful move which ended with Bobby Smith sidefooting a pass from Greaves into the net.

But Czechoslovakia wouldn't lie down. Scherer pulled a goal back with a fine header and three minutes later it could have been 2–2. Bubernik hit the bar with a shot that deserved a goal. The ball rebounded to Kvasnak and, believe it or not, his shot hit the bar as well.

That was the lucky break England needed and Bobby Charlton raced through to make it 3–1. Once again the home side hit back and Kadraba scored with a flying header. But Jimmy Greaves sealed it for England with a goal even cheekier than his first. With only ten minutes left he took a pass from Paine, juggled with the ball, flicked it over his head, turned and rammed it home. It was the best England display for a long time and the players thoroughly deserved their standing ovation at the end.

After this satisfying victory the England party travelled to Leipzig confident they could complete the tour undefeated. In a hard-fought match on 2 June against East Germany, Roger Hunt, of Liverpool, winning his second cap, scored the opening goal and Bobby Charlton added the second to give England a 2–1 win.

So it was off to Basle, the Swiss city on the border of France and Germany, and a right old romp it turned out to be.

Believing that every one in the travelling party should get at least one game, Alf Ramsey made seven changes from the side which had beaten East Germany three days earlier. Ron Flowers, of Wolves, took the place of Maurice Norman, Ron Springett, of Sheffield Wednesday, took over in goal from Gordon Banks and the forward line was completely remodelled.

Only Bobby Charlton kept his place. Terry Paine, Roger Hunt, Bobby Smith and George Eastham made way for Bryan Douglas, Jimmy Greaves, Johnny Byrne (for his second cap but his first since moving from West Ham United to Crystal Palace) and Jimmy Melia.

The seventh change was Tony Kay, of Everton, taking over the No. 4 shirt from Gordon Milne. And what a début he had! Rarely has anyone started his international career in such tremendous style. He towered over everyone like a red-haired giant. One second he was tackling strongly in defence, the next he was up in attack. He made two goals, scored one himself and almost broke the crossbar with a shot of frightening ferocity. If they had given such awards as Man of the Match in those days, Tony Kay would have won it in a canter.

I said at the time that I couldn't imagine a future England side without him, but sadly we were to see no more of Tony Kay on the international scene. He was involved in a case of match-fixing and a highly promising career disintegrated.

The final score in Basle was 8–1, England's biggest win since that never-to-be-forgotten day at Wembley when England beat Scotland 9–3 in April 1961. Jimmy Greaves scored three times against the Scots, but he didn't get one against the Swiss. Fancy an 8–1 win without Greaves getting at least one of the goals! Bobby Charlton, with three, was the goalscorer in chief at Basle, ably assisted by Johnny Byrne, who scored twice and Bryan Douglas, Jimmy Melia and Tony Kay who chipped in with a goal apiece.

The whole party celebrated an outstanding end to a tour which had given England a one hundred per cent record.

At last the England team were on the right track and the stuttering start of the Alf Ramsey regime was but a bad memory.

After the defeat by Scotland at Wembley on 6 April 1963 until they lined up at Wembley against Uruguay in the opening game of the World Cup on 11 July 1966, England played thirty-six internationals, twenty-four of which were won, eight drawn and only four lost – against Scotland, Brazil, Argentina and Austria. England scored ninety-four goals and conceded forty-one.

During that splendid run, England toured South America and met all the best sides in Europe – Austria, West Germany, Yugoslavia, Spain and the like.

So the record was one of which the team and the manager could be justly proud. But even so, very few people in England believed England would win the World Cup.

English football fans are born pessimists and groaners, led more often than not by the media. Many were quick to point out that we had been knocked out of the European Championships, so what hope did we have against the world? The victories in Czechoslovakia, East Germany and Switzerland were written off as meaningless wins against weak opposition by those who thought it was fashionable to decry England's efforts.

But Alf Ramsey believed and perhaps that is what tipped the scales in our favour.

Admittedly, there were serious problems ahead. As hosts, we automatically qualified for the final stages of the World Cup, and thus had to make do with friendly matches for the next three years. There was an advantage in this insofar as friendly games allowed experiments to be made with the team, but on the other side of the coin was the fact that friendly games lacked the bite of real competition and tended to fudge the importance of the results.

There were also the self-made problems because little or nothing was done by the authorities to allow the England squad to get together for training sessions. Clubs, too, did not help the situation with their reluctance to release players for international duties. The club versus country debate was a heated one then. Clubs usually won.

I remember interviewing the chairman of a First Division club (in pre-Premiership days) and asking him whether, given the choice, he would prefer his club to win the League Championship or England to win the World Cup. The reply was, 'My club to win the Championship.'

He claimed that the fans agreed with him, and he was right. The average football fans are dedicated to the team they support. The fate of the national side is something that doesn't really touch their hearts. A defeat for their local side is a bitter blow to their pride. A defeat for the national side is easily shrugged off with the claim that 'if they'd picked our centre forward they would have won'.

The national team manager has to struggle against such attitudes as well as apply himself to the problems over which he has some control. These are baffling enough. With three seasons to go before the 1966 Finals, Alf Ramsey had to wonder how many of his tried and trusted internationals would be past their best come July 1966. And he had to search for the emerging young players who might be ready to burst on to the scene and make an impact by then. All that in three years and just thirty-two games, ten fewer than the teams were then playing in a season.

2

The Patient Build-up

1963–64 season

The first test in the three-season build-up came at Ninian Park, Cardiff, against Wales on 12 October 1963. It seemed an age since that eight-goal jamboree in Basle, and when the team was announced it contained six changes from the one which had annihilated the Swiss. Out went Springett, Kay, Flowers, Douglas, Byrne and Melia; in came Banks, Milne, Norman, Paine, Bobby Smith and Eastham.

England took the field in Cardiff represented by Banks (Leicester City); Armfield (Blackpool), captain, Wilson (Huddersfield Town); Milne (Liverpool), Norman (Tottenham Hotspur), Moore (West Ham United); Paine (Southampton), Greaves (Tottenham Hotspur), Smith (Tottenham Hotspur), Eastham (Arsenal), Charlton (Manchester United).

England got off to a great start when Smith scored after only four minutes, but it was the final goal of the 4–0 England win which raised the biggest cheer of the day. It was scored eight minutes from the end by Bobby Charlton. It was his thirty-first goal for his country, one more than both Tom Finney and Nat Lofthouse.

Nineteen sixty-three was the centenary of the Football Association and, as part of the celebrations a match had been arranged at Wembley against a Rest of the World XI. The big occasion came eleven days after the win in Wales.

When they settled down to pick the Rest of the World team FIFA were faced with an embarrassment of riches so they chose sixteen players and stipulated that they would all play some part of the match. The Rest of the World lined up for the first half with: Yashin (Soviet Union); Djalma Santos (Brazil), Schnellinger (West Germany); Pluskal, Popluhar and Masopust (all from Czechoslovakia); Kopa (France), Law (Scotland), Di Stefano (Spain), Eusébio (Portugal) and Gento (Spain). England took the field with the team that had beaten Wales.

There were changes at half-time. Soskic (Yugoslavia) replaced Yashin in goal, Eyzaguirre (Chile) was at right back in place of Santos, Baxter (Scotland) came on instead of Masopust, and Puskas (Hungarian-born but now playing for Spain) took over from Eusébio. With half an hour to go, Uwe Seeler, who was to captain West Germany in the 1966 World Cup Final, replaced Kopa.

It was a day to remember with so many truly great players providing a feast of football entertainment for the 100,000 spectators who paid £90,000 for the privilege of being there. (If Wembley could accommodate 100,000 spectators today, the gate receipts would be between three and four million pounds!)

Anyone who was lucky enough to be there has their own memory of the game, but mine concerned Jimmy Greaves and Lev Yashin, who tied for the title of my Man of the Match. In the last minute of the first half, Greaves broke through the middle. Actually, the half-time whistle went before he could shoot, but Greaves kept going and released a real piledriver. With a grin as wide as his face, Yashin just flicked his right fist and brushed the ball aside. The two players walked off with their arms around each other.

For the record England won 2–1 with goals from Paine and Charlton to one from Law and the teams left the field to a standing ovation by the capacity crowd.

This feast of football played in a splendid spirit had proved that England could compete at the highest level against some of the greatest players in the world. Not surprisingly, therefore, Alf Ramsey chose the same side for the next historic occasion, except for the selection of Wolverhampton's Thompson at left back in place of the injured Wilson.

It was hard to think of an international against Northern Ireland as a historic occasion until the Wednesday evening of 20 November 1963 when it became the first international played at Wembley under floodlights. The crowds didn't roll up – only 45,000 of them turned out – but then we all know how difficult it is to get to Wembley, especially for an evening kick-off. Those who stayed away missed an excellent England performance and four goals from Jimmy Greaves in a very satisfying 8–3 win.

England were on a roll, but suddenly all momentum was lost as the next international – against Scotland at Hampden Park – was five months away. International sides need plenty of match practice if they are to develop the team understanding so necessary for success at the highest level. An awful lot can happen in five months, as many national team managers have found to their cost.

11 April 1964 was not a day to remember at Hampden Park. The wind blew and the rain fell, in contrast to the rest of Britain where the sun shone. So it was a pretty miserable

afternoon for the 134,000 spectators, although the Scots did have the consolation of seeing their team win 1–0.

It was England's first defeat for a year, since, in fact, they had lost 2–1 at Wembley, also to Scotland, and it was particularly disappointing as only three changes had been made to the side which had thrashed Northern Ireland at Wembley the previous November. Ray Wilson, recovered from his injury, had returned at left back and Roger Hunt and Johnny Byrne had come into the attack in place of Jimmy Greaves and Bobby Smith.

During the close season England faced a stiff test. Uruguay were coming to Wembley and then followed games in Portugal, the Republic of Ireland and the United States before a visit to Brazil to take part in the Little World Cup, a quadrangular tournament with Argentina, Brazil and Portugal.

The game against Uruguay at Wembley on 6 May 1964 excited nobody. It was a scratch Uruguayan side which had scraped through 1–0 against Morocco and then lost 3–0 to Northern Ireland. Furthermore, Nacional and Peñarol, the clubs which normally formed the backbone of any Uruguayan national team, only provided one player each for this occasion. Yet England had to struggle to a narrow win by just 2–1.

There was only one bright spot in the match – the international début of George Cohen, the Fulham right back, in a team of Banks; Cohen, Wilson; Milne, Norman, Moore (captain); Paine, Greaves, Byrne, Eastham, Charlton. Cohen gave a splendid display, but little did we realize that we had just witnessed the start of a brilliant international career which was to remain unbroken, except for two games, until 1967.

Johnny Byrne scored both the goals against Uruguay and went one better in Portugal on 17 May by scoring a hat-trick against the Portuguese in a 4–3 win.

A week later we were in Dublin with an unchanged team with the exception that Ron Flowers played alongside Bobby Moore at the heart of the defence instead of Maurice Norman, and Tony Waiters took over in goal from Gordon Banks. Johnny Byrne, nicknamed 'Budgie' because he never stopped talking (and he still doesn't!) scored his usual goal and Eastham and Greaves added one each to make it a 3–1 win.

Alf took the opportunity of giving some fresh players a run for the game with the United States in New York, and the team was Banks (Leicester City); Cohen (Fulham), Bob Thompson (Wolves); Bailey (Charlton Athletic), Norman (Tottenham Hotspur), Flowers (Wolves) captain; Paine (Southampton), Hunt (Liverpool), Pickering (Blackburn Rovers), Eastham (Arsenal), Peter Thompson (Liverpool).

England set off on the road to Rio with a 10–0 victory safely under their belt with goals from Hunt (4), Pickering (3), Paine (2) and Charlton.

The overture was finished. Now started the real performance and England had the privilege of opening the Little World Cup tournament with a match against the hosts, Brazil.

The England players soon found out what international football in Brazil involved. The team coach was escorted to the giant Maracaná Stadium by a posse of acrobatic policemen on motorcycles doing handstands on the handlebars, standing on the seats with hands not touching any of the controls. They could have been performers in a brilliant circus act! All along the route to the stadium people cheered the English squad.

Nothing had prepared the English players for what came next. Kick-off time approached and the players lined up ready to take the field: Waiters (Blackpool); Cohen (Fulham),

Wilson (Huddersfield Town); Milne (Liverpool), Norman (Tottenham Hotspur), Moore (West Ham United) captain; Thompson (Liverpool), Greaves (Tottenham Hotspur), Byrne (West Ham United), Eastham (Arsenal), Charlton (Manchester United).

They were ready for the off but the Brazilians weren't. Time means nothing to Brazilians. I remember once being invited to lunch at the exclusive Rio Yacht Club by a very well-respected citizen. One o'clock he had said. I arrived on time but there was no sign of my host. Well aware of the Brazilians' lack of punctuality I tried to be patient, and just after two o'clock the gentleman arrived. There was a friendly greeting but not a word of apology or explanation. Lateness is not a crime in Rio!

Nor was it a crime at the Maracana. Everybody waited patiently until the Brazilian team appeared and the game got under way more than an hour and a half late.

It was distracting for the England players, worrying for the journalists who had to make deadlines, but the Brazilian performance was well worth the wait.

Brazil won the match 5–1, which suggests an embarrassing thrashing for the English. But it was nothing of the sort. England were beaten by a genius and by an inspired spell during the second half which brought Brazil three goals in eight minutes. The genius was Pelé.

Pelé was the mastermind who took the game by the scruff of the neck and bent it to his will. In a display of sheer brilliance which had us all spellbound, he scored one goal, was involved in two others and the fifth and final goal resulted from a free-kick awarded after he had been brought down with only Waiters to beat. Pelé's goal came when he took a return pass from Vává and placed a glorious twenty-five-yard shot just wide of Waiters.

But England, although soundly beaten, were not dis-
graced. They were a goal down at half-time, but when
Greaves equalized in the first minute of the second half,
there were reasonable expectations that England could bring
off a surprise victory. Then came those three goals in eight
minutes and it was all over.

The next match was against Portugal in São Paulo, and
after a fine display against Brazil, English hopes were high. It
turned out to be an anti-climax. The two sides produced a
drab, dreary display which ended 1–1 and made certain that
only a sensational England win over Argentina could rob the
South Americans of first place in the tournament.

There was never any real danger of that. Argentina won
1–0 and finished the tournament with a one hundred percent
record and not having conceded a goal, following up a 2–0
win over Portugal with a 3–0 drubbing of Brazil in a bad-
tempered game in São Paulo. England, like Portugal, were
left to contemplate that it is mighty tough at the top.

But the English players had won a lot of friends, especially
among the youngsters of Rio, highly skilled at playing in
bare feet on soft sand, who challenged them to a game on
Copacabana Beach. One England player found it hard.

He was the object of a hard though fair tackle, but,
unaccustomed as he was to beach football, he limped away
with a very sore toe. He was in such discomfort that it was
thought prudent to take him to a doctor, who diagnosed a
break. But, although all the members of the media covering
the tour were present – some of us even played too – not a
word was printed in any newspaper or broadcast on any
radio or television station. It was as if the incident had never
happened. After all, the team was on the eve of a return
home with no more games to play until the new season,
when our casualty would have made a full recovery (he did),

so why make a fuss? In those days there was a mutual trust and respect between players and reporters, which sadly does not seem to exist today. Nothing was going to be allowed to spoil the goodwill the players had built up by having a kick-about on the beach with the Rio children, all of whom were passionate about the game of football and their idols who played it.

As we all set off home from Rio de Janeiro, we began to consider the first eighteen months of Alf Ramsey's reign as manager. The record was:

	Played	Won	Drawn	Lost	For	Against	Points	Percentage
Home	5	3	1	1	14	8	10	66.6
Away	12	7	1	4	39	21	22	61.1
Total	17	10	2	5	53	29	32	62.8

Note: The points totals have been worked out using the modern system of three points for a win.

You could make out a good report from a record like that one. Over three goals a match scored, well under two goals a match conceded, with a points return of 62.8 percent with two-thirds of the games being played away from home.

(In hindsight, of course, we can point out too that Banks, Cohen, Wilson, Moore, Hunt and Bobby Charlton – all six of whom were in the World Cup Final winning side of 1966 – were by now firmly established in the squad. So we were getting somewhere. . . .)

But the knockers told a different story. Much of the opposition had been weak and the goal total was flattered by the ten goals against the United States and the eight scored against both Northern Ireland and Switzerland. When we had come up against the big boys we had lost – to Argentina, to Brazil, to France (in the important European Championships) and to

Scotland, not once but twice. Although the English have never been as fanatical about the England–Scotland encounters as the Scots are, two defeats in a row was too much for the average fan to stomach.

1964–65 season

Besides the three Home Internationals – against Scotland, Wales and Northern Ireland – two other autumn games had been arranged against strong opposition: Belgium and Holland. At the end of the season a home game against Hungary was scheduled, followed by a tour to Yugoslavia, West Germany and Sweden. The pressure on the players was being increased.

Many people accused Alf Ramsey of picking teams which were 'wingless wonders', so it is significant that in all but one of the internationals this season Alf selected two wingmen. First it was Paine (on the right) and Peter Thompson (on the left) against Northern Ireland; then Peter Thompson (on the right) and Alan Hinton against Belgium and Wales; followed by Peter Thompson and Bobby Charlton (on the left wing, his original position when he broke into the game) against Holland and also against Scotland; finally, Paine and Connelly against Hungary, Yugoslavia and Sweden. The odd game out was against West Germany in Nuremberg, where Paine was the only recognized wingman . . . although a little fellow by the name of Alan Ball came into the side to win his second cap.

Of those nine internationals, five were won and four were drawn, with a goal total of 16–11. The draws came against Belgium, Holland, Scotland and Yugoslavia.

Perhaps the most important result was the victory in Nuremberg over West Germany, who were rightly regarded as one of the finest sides in Europe. Terry Paine scored the only goal of the match and Alf Ramsey had a satisfied smile on his face at the end. Honest, he did.

By now, not only Alan Ball but also Nobby Stiles and Jack Charlton had established themselves in the England plans. Nine of the future World Champions were in the side and England had gone a year without defeat.

England's record under Ramsey was now:

	Played	Won	Drawn	Lost	For	Against	Points	Percentage
Home	9	5	3	1	21	13	18	66.6
Away	17	10	3	4	48	27	33	64.7
Total	26	15	6	5	69	40	51	65.4

1965–66 season

The big test was looming up on the horizon. As the season began there was less than twelve months before the start of the World Cup, less than twelve months for Alf Ramsey to get his squad of twenty-two firmly settled in his mind, not to mention what he would regard as his best eleven.

Determined to give all the 'possibles' a test, and a severe one, Alf arranged eight games between October and May, which would be followed by a pre-tournament tour to Scandinavia and Poland.

Ron Springett, who hadn't been in the side since that 8–1 victory over Switzerland in Basle in June 1963, was chosen to keep goal against Wales in Cardiff on 2 October 1965. Again Alf chose two wingmen – Paine and Connelly – for this match and for the following one against Austria at Wembley later the same month. The game against Wales was goalless, but Austria won at Wembley by three goals to two.

Two wingmen were also picked for the match against Northern Ireland at Wembley – Peter Thompson replaced

Paine – and although England won 2–1 there was a complete change of thinking for the next international against Spain in Madrid on 8 December. Out went the wingers and England adopted a 4–3–3 formation with Ball, Stiles and Eastham in the midfield, and Bobby Charlton up front with Joe Baker and Roger Hunt. The rest of the team had what was to become a familiar look about it with Banks in goal, and Cohen, Jack Charlton, Moore and Wilson in the back four. Everything went smoothly and Spain were beaten even more comprehensively than the score of 2–0 suggests.

And so we entered the fateful year of 1966 with Alf Ramsey able to look back on a record of:

	Played	Won	Drawn	Lost	For	Against	Points	Percentage
Home	11	6	3	2	25	17	21	63.6
Away	19	11	4	4	50	27	37	65.0
Total	30	17	7	6	75	44	58	64.4

Was this a good enough record to win the World Cup? Would a side winning just over half its matches be good enough against the very top class opposition? A number of people thought not.

3

Final Preparations

As we entered 1966, World Cup year, it did not seem to me that the nation was gripped with World Cup fever. There wasn't a great air of optimism about, despite the good results the team had produced under the guidance of Alf Ramsey. Many people seemed to be worrying about the so-called 'really good teams', popularly believed to be West Germany, Portugal, Argentina and Brazil. (History would later show that England beat them all, except Brazil. And they didn't last long enough to qualify for a game against England.)

One man remained convinced that England would win the World Cup – Alf Ramsey. He had said it right from the start of his reign and he was never averse to repeating his forecast. What the pessimists didn't know was that Alf had managed to instil his confidence into all the players he had chosen since his appointment. They had grown to believe in their leader and to believe in themselves.

A tough run-in had been arranged: Poland (oh, how the Poles keep bobbing up in our World Cup history!), West Germany (what a superb piece of clairvoyance that turned out to be), Scotland, three Scandinavian countries and then Poland once again, this time in Chorzhow. There could hardly have been a stiffer seven-match test. England won six of those matches, the only blemish (if you can call it that) being a 1–1 draw in the first meeting with Poland on 7 January. Once again England fielded the side which Alf apparently believed was his best, with the exception of Harris playing in place of Bobby Charlton. But it was not good enough to win against a country which has become England's bogey team.

The big test came at Wembley on 23 February 1966 when, on a wet and windy night, England entertained West Germany. Many of the 75,000 spectators who braved the weather must have scratched their heads in bewilderment when the England line-up was announced. It was, in its 4–3–3 formation: Banks (Leicester City); Cohen (Fulham), Jack Charlton (Leeds United), Moore (West Ham United) captain, Newton (Blackburn Rovers); Stiles (Manchester United), Hunter (Leeds United), Bobby Charlton (Manchester United); Ball (Blackpool), Hunt (Liverpool), Hurst (West Ham United).

What threw the fans was the fact that Nobby Stiles was wearing the No. 9 shirt, and while they were wondering what sort of a centre forward he would make, they didn't really notice the man wearing the No. 10 shirt – Geoff Hurst making his first appearance for England. So England, whatever the fans thought, were near to their best side, the one that would win the trophy. True, three newcomers (Hurst, Hunter and Newton, who was carried off with a leg injury after forty-three minutes, just two minutes after Stiles had scored the only goal of the match) were introduced, but of the eleven who finished the game (Wilson having come on for the injured Newton), only Norman Hunter did not play in the Final. He was, though, a member of the squad of twenty-two.

Strangely enough (in view of what would happen in the Final), there was a was-the-ball-over-the-line-or-wasn't-it controversy. A quarter of an hour before the end the Germans scored what they and the spectators thought was a magnificent goal. Ziggy Held, who was making his début for the Germans, reached the ball on the by-line.

Well, did he reach it on the by-line or before the by-line, as everybody thought? Certainly he chipped the ball into the middle of the penalty area with great accuracy and Heiss volleyed it with such force that Banks didn't even move as the ball flashed past him into the back of the net. The Germans – and the spectators – celebrated a splendid goal. The English players made no protest, not, that is, until Ray Wilson saw the linesman with his flag held high in the air. The referee went over to consult him, and changed his decision from a goal to a goal kick. The linesman had reported that the ball was over the line before Held centred.

So England won 1–0 and the players must have been shattered as their exit from the field was the signal for boos, jeers and slow handclapping. The fans had been bored by a tactical battle fought mainly in midfield, though the tussle between two teams which seemed determined to be there or thereabouts when the big prize was handed out on 30 July was nothing like as uninteresting as some people made it out to be. Fans do not appreciate the finer points of tactical battles. What they want is a whole-hearted, thrill-a-minute set-to. But this was a warm-up for the World Cup Finals, a game between two equally matched teams who wanted to give nothing away. Now, just a few months before the start of the really serious stuff, was no time for thinking in terms of pure entertainment.

The Germans were at the same stage of their preparation as the English, and they used this game as a chance to experiment. Only five of the side they fielded at Wembley played in the Final in June.

There was no Uwe Seeler, no Karl-Heinz Schnellinger, no Helmut Haller. So nobody got carried away by yet another victory. It was, perhaps, a good thing that Alf Ramsey was such an experienced campaigner not to be upset by the whingers claiming that, although everything wasn't wrong, there was more wrong than right. Other managers of the national side have faced a similar lack of confidence from the fans. Times don't change. . . .

The next test was reserved for Glasgow's Hampden Park on 2 April, when England faced their old rivals, the country which seemed to have the Indian sign on them – Scotland. Ramsey decided to give another run out to Keith Newton, now happily recovered from the injury he had sustained against West Germany, and once again an out-and-out winger was chosen – Manchester United's John Connelly. England won the match 4–3, but it was not as close as the scoreline seems to indicate. England were much the better side and Alf Ramsey must have been delighted at the splendid way Hunt and Hurst combined. Both scored – Hunt twice – and Bobby Charlton got the fourth. Altogether it was a performance to send the English supporters away happy.

A month later – on 7 May – it was back to Wembley for the last time before the World Cup. The opponents were Yugoslavia and the cynics were quick to point out that the Yugoslavs had failed to qualify for the final stages of the World Cup so England should expect a comfortable victory. Furthermore, four members of the Yugoslav team were due to play in the following week's European Cup Final and their thoughts would be on that rather than on a friendly international.

Alf Ramsey must have been thinking along similar lines because he took the opportunity to experiment and gave players on the fringe of the squad eleventh-hour chances to show what they could do. Out went Cohen, Moore, Newton, Ball, Hunt and Connelly; in came Jimmy Armfield, to take over the captaincy, Ray Wilson, Norman Hunter, Terry Paine, Jimmy Greaves (for the first time after a seven-month lay-off with jaundice) and Bobby Tambling, of Chelsea, for the first time since that 5–2 defeat in Paris, Alf Ramsey's first match in charge, way back in February 1963. There was one other change from the side which had played Scotland. Nobby Stiles was left out and in his place there was a new cap – another West Ham United star, Martin Peters.

It was another filthy night at Wembley – pouring rain – but it did nothing to dampen the spirits of the England players. True, there were some shaky moments in defence. True, there were missed chances. But there was a victory, with a goal from Greaves (a header, believe it or not) and another from Charlton (one of those twenty-five-yard left-foot specials he delivered every now and then to the delight of everyone except the opposing goalkeeper).

And so England set off in June on the last lap of their pre-paration for the final stages of one of the biggest, if not THE biggest single-sport extravaganza. A tour prior to such an important competition was the ideal opportunity to develop the camaraderie so vital to the squad, and to work on various aspects of the game far from the gaze of the home supporters and the pressures of competitive football.

First stop was Helsinki to play Finland, where football is not the most popular sport. In fact, at that time the stan-dard of their national side was about on a par with the old Second Division in England. Finland had recently suffered two defeats at the hands of Israel, 0–3 at home and 1–7 in Israel.

England, it seemed, were in for little more than a leisurely training run, a belief further strengthened by the fact that Finland selected five Second Division players.

It was, however, not the time for England to worry about the difficulties their opponents might be having. England were on the eve of the biggest test in the history of English football and they had to treat all opponents as if they were world champions.

So Alf didn't tinker with the defence, which remained the same as against Yugoslavia. Banks was the goalkeeper behind a back four of Armfield, Jack Charlton, Hunter and Wilson. Ball, Bobby Charlton and Peters were in midfield with Ian Callaghan as the wingman supporting Hurst and Hunt up front. Callaghan, incidentally, was making his début. Alf was still fine-tuning his midfield and attack and World Cup places were still available.

Cally rose to the occasion and had an excellent first match in an England shirt, but England's performance was little to shout about. Against poor opposition they were never likely to concede a goal, but it was worrying to see so many chances, including a penalty, going astray.

The game was killed by two goals in as many minutes almost on half-time. Both goals were examples of good club cooperation. After forty-two minutes it was West Ham's turn: Hurst centred and Peters headed home. Two minutes later the Liverpool connection struck, Hunt heading home Callaghan's centre. We had to wait until the last minute of the match for the third goal, which seemed a bit of a fluky one. Jack Charlton centred from the by-line and the ball bounced into the net off a Finnish defender. Ah well, they all count! But once again the overall performance didn't attract rave notices.

Three days later it was Norway who provided the opposition in Oslo's sunlit Ulleval Stadium. Once again there were wholesale changes in the England side so that the opportunities could be evenly spread. Springett took over in goal, and the back four was Cohen, Flowers, Moore and Gerry Byrne, of Liverpool, playing his first international for three years. The midfield was left to the Manchester United pair of Stiles and Bobby Charlton, and two wingmen, Paine on the right and Connelly on the left, were up front alongside Hunt and Greaves.

There was a big question mark about Jimmy Greaves. No one doubted that he had been one of the world's most lethal goal scorers, but the operative words were 'had been'. Jimmy was by now clear of the jaundice which had kept him out of the team for so long but the debilitating disease had taken a severe toll and he seemed tired and lifeless.

Though there was nothing unusual in that, since the effects of jaundice can linger on for six months or more, the crucial question was, 'Will Jimmy Greaves be fit enough to play in the World Cup Finals?' There were many who would have answered 'No' to that question ... until they went to the Ulleval Stadium in Oslo on 29 June 1966.

It was there, at long last, that we saw the real Jimmy Greaves again. Norway at that time were not the tough opposition they became in later years, but even so they did give England a torrid time for the first twenty minutes, during which England were all at sixes and sevens, and even went a goal down after four minutes when Sunde intercepted a back pass which never looked like reaching Springett.

Then, in the twentieth minute, Greavsie took over. He flung himself through the air to meet a centre from Hunt and headed the ball into the net with the force and accuracy of a Dean, a Lawton or a Lofthouse. Headed goals were not

Greaves's usual forte. Quick bursts down the middle were, and just to prove it he set off on one almost as soon as the Norwegians had kicked off after the equalizing goal. His speed off the mark left the Norwegian defence standing, and he raced forty yards with the ball at his feet, three or four defenders chasing him but always looking as if they were going to finish second. When the goalkeeper began to advance in an attempt to narrow the angle, Greaves slotted the ball home.

It was an electrifying goal, as spectacular as his headed one just sixty seconds previously. What is more, letting in two goals inside a minute made the Norwegians start to crumble.

Two minutes later the Norwegian collapse was complete when Connelly scored to put England 3–1 ahead. By now England could do what they liked, and even Bobby Moore got into the act five minutes from half-time, scoring the fourth goal with a superb shot from fully twenty-five yards. Two minutes from half-time, the Norwegian goalkeeper and Connelly collided. The ball ran loose so Greaves tapped it into the empty net to complete his hat-trick and put the game completely out of Norway's reach with England relaxing with a 5–1 lead. In case there was any sign of a Norwegian revival, Greaves rattled in yet another goal on the hour to give England a resounding 6–1 victory and dispel all doubts about his fitness.

As the England party prepared to leave the Bristol Hotel in Oslo on the morning of Friday, 1 July for the last leg of the Scandinavian tour, Joe Mears, Chairman of the Football Association, collapsed and died from a heart attack. Joe, who was also Chairman of Chelsea, had set his heart on seeing England win the World Cup, but fate decreed that he would never fulfil his ambition. He was struck down just twenty-nine days before the Final triumph.

Despite the tragedy it was decided that the game in Copenhagen on 3 July had to go on. Denmark were seeking their first win for a year. In fact, they had lost at home to Norway the previous Sunday, the same Norway that finished 6–1 losers to England three days later.

We awaited with great interest Alf Ramsey's team selection for this penultimate game before the World Cup and, as usual, he gave us a surprise: he handed a first cap to Peter Bonetti, the Chelsea goalkeeper. He got his place behind what was now obviously the preferred back four of Cohen, Jack Charlton, Moore and Wilson. Stiles, Ball and Eastham were in midfield, with Connelly on the wing and Greaves and Hurst the front runners. It was Jimmy Greaves' fiftieth appearance for England, and before the kick-off the Danish Football Association presented him with a piece of Copenhagen porcelain.

Perhaps it was as a 'thank you' that he didn't score. In fact nobody found goalscoring easy, in a low-key match, shrouded in sadness because of Joe Mears' death. Jack Charlton, with a fine header, set England on the road to victory two minutes before half-time, and midway through the second half the Danish goalkeeper allowed a simple shot to slip through his fingers into the net to give a final score of 2–0.

It was England's eighth victory in their last nine internationals, but it still didn't fill everyone with great confidence. As I waited to board a London-bound aircraft at Copenhagen airport the day following the match, a senior Football Association official said to me, 'We'll win nothing with that fellow in charge.'

All I could think of as a reply was, 'Well, you and your colleagues appointed him and it's too late to sack him now so we will just have to hope for the best.'

After that short conversation we travelled together to

London, he, no doubt, to spread doom and gloom among everyone he met, and I to introduce a World Cup preview programme for BBC Television. Meanwhile, 'that fellow in charge' was winging his way to Poland with those footballers who hadn't a chance of winning us the World Cup.

Nevertheless, on 5 July 1966 in Chorzhow those footballers, or at least eleven of them, beat Poland by the only goal of the match, scored by Roger Hunt. And the team that day? It was: Banks (Leicester City); Cohen (Fulham), Jack Charlton (Leeds United), Moore (West Ham United), captain, Wilson (Huddersfield Town); Ball (Blackpool), Stiles (Manchester United), Bobby Charlton (Manchester United), Peters (West Ham United); Greaves (Tottenham Hotspur), Hunt (Liverpool).

Someone, somewhere had made his mind up!

4

The England Squad

The time soon came for the man who seemed to have made his mind up to announce to the world the twenty-two players he believed could and would win the World Cup for England. His record since taking over as manager had been good, according to some, and dodgy, according to others, depending on how you interpreted the results.

Alf Ramsey finally announced his squad and a well-balanced squad it appeared to be. There were three goal-keepers, eight defenders, eight midfield players (including three orthodox wingers) and three acknowledged strikers. The names of the twenty-two English standard bearers were:

GOALKEEPERS: Gordon Banks (Leicester City), Peter Bonetti (Chelsea) and Ron Springett (Sheffield Wednesday).

DEFENDERS: Jimmy Armfield (Blackpool), Gerry Byrne (Liverpool), Jack Charlton (Leeds United), George Cohen (Fulham), Ron Flowers (Wolverhampton Wanderers), Norman Hunter (Leeds United), Bobby Moore (West Ham United), captain, Ray Wilson (Huddersfield Town).

MIDFIELD: Alan Ball (Blackpool), Ian Callaghan (Liverpool), Bobby Charlton (Manchester United), John Connelly (Manchester United), George Eastham (Arsenal), Terry Paine (Southampton), Martin Peters (West Ham United), Nobby Stiles (Manchester United).
STRIKERS: Jimmy Greaves (Tottenham Hotspur), Roger Hunt (Liverpool), Geoff Hurst (West Ham United).

It was a squad which varied in experience from the sixty-eight caps of Bobby Charlton to the single caps of Peter Bonetti and Ian Callaghan. Four other players were in single figures: Gerry Byrne (two), Martin Peters (three), Norman Hunter (four) and Geoff Hurst (five). It was also a versatile squad, with a number of players able to play in more than one position, giving Alf Ramsey the option to vary his tactics. If, for instance, none of the three wingers clicked, Bobby Charlton could well be played in a wide role.

One thing Alf Ramsey could rightly boast about was that he had three of the world's finest players in his squad. They were Bobby Charlton, Bobby Moore and the goalkeeper, Gordon Banks.

Banks began his career with Chesterfield, but after only twenty-three games for them he was transferred to Leicester City, where he gained most of his fame. He was twenty-seven and had won twenty-seven caps by the time he took the field against Uruguay in the World Cup's opening game, and he won his seventy-third and final cap in 1972, the year his career ended abruptly after he lost an eye in a car crash while a Stoke City player.

On his retirement he formed his own sports promotion company. As so many other famous sportsmen, he combines his professional activity with frequent forays into the field of after-dinner speaking.

Of the other two goalkeepers in the squad, Peter Bonetti had won a single cap – against Denmark in Copenhagen just before the World Cup began, while Ron Springett was much more experienced, with thirty-three caps to his name. Bonetti went on to win seven caps altogether, the last coming in the 1970 World Cup match in Leon when West Germany turned a 0–2 scoreline into a 3–2 victory. Springett, by then at the end of his career, was never called upon after the 1966 World Cup. He had, however, played in all England's games in the 1962 World Cup in Chile, a run which ended at the quarter-final stage.

When Springett retired he concentrated on his sports outfitter's business, though he later sold it to go back to his trade of building and decorating. But he still played often for the teams of veterans Bobby Charlton took on tours. 'In fact,' Ron said, 'I visited more places with Bob's team of old-timers than I did with Queen's Park Rangers, Sheffield Wednesday and England.'

Ron still keeps a lively interest in today's game and is often to be seen at Loftus Road watching one of his old teams, Queen's Park Rangers. His daughter, Terry, is the Rangers' Assistant Secretary and she always reminds Ron of a great day in his life.

Terry was born on 15 April 1961, making her first appearance just two hours before kick-off time for the England and Scotland international at Wembley. Ron was in goal for England that day and received news of Terry's arrival not long before he walked out on to the pitch. His team-mates decided to turn it into a real celebration by beating Scotland 9–3, and that victory set Ron off on a run of twenty-one consecutive appearances in the England goal.

What of the defence? Jimmy Armfield was, perhaps, the surprise choice. He had been capped forty-three times and was thirty years of age, but while some people might have thought he was past his sell-by date, Alf Ramsey knew that Jimmy Armfield was not only a class player but also a wonderful man to have around the dressing-room. If spirits needed keeping up, Armfield was the man to do it.

He never played for England during or after the 1966 World Cup, but his 43 caps say enough about his international class. His 568 appearances for Blackpool, his only club, testify to his loyalty. He was still with Blackpool, his home town, when he retired as a player in 1971 and took over as manager of Bolton Wanderers for three seasons.

The media then beckoned and he gained a high reputation as a BBC radio reporter and analyst, and also as a *Daily Express* sports writer.

When, in 1993, Graham Taylor's time as England manager came to a close and the Football Association were keen to sign a top-class successor who could take charge of England into Europe 96, they lured Jimmy Armfield away from the media and asked him to make some suggestions.

Jimmy proposed that the job title should be changed from England manager to England coach, and gave his opinion that one man stood head and shoulders above all the many candidates for the job – Terry Venables. Terry was appointed, and by then Jimmy Armfield had proved himself too valuable an asset to lose. He accepted the offer of the job of the Football Association's Technical Consultant, which means that since 1993 he has advised the FA on a whole range of technical matters, and he has also worked closely with Don Howe at The Football School of Excellence at Lilleshall.

For an ordinary person that would be enough, but Jim is no ordinary person. In addition to working long hours and travelling long distances in his football work, he still finds time to be a school governor and a vice-president of

Outward Bound. And to keep himself occupied in his spare time he plays the organ at his local church every Sunday, just as he has done for the last twenty-five years.

While Jimmy Armfield is still wrapped up in football, Gerry Byrne, the former Liverpool full back, hardly ever goes to a game these days. 'Mind you,' he told me, 'I watch it on television and I must admit that I get the odd twitch of excitement and the urge to get stuck into a tackle or make a raid down the wing. But then I realize all good things must come to an end.'

Perhaps all good things do come to an end, but Gerry Byrne's enthusiasm can never die, judging by the way he performed on 1 May 1965 in the FA Cup Final. Liverpool played Leeds United and in the second minute Byrne was tackled by Leeds' Bobby Collins. He seemed to recover all right, but I noticed that even after treatment he kept his right arm tucked very tightly into his side. I mentioned this in my commentary and assumed that something was wrong and that Byrne was in pain.

It transpired later that he had broken his collar bone in that second-minute incident and yet he played on to the bitter end. And the bitter end didn't come until after extra-time with Liverpool 2–1 winners, their first-ever FA Cup Final victory.

Players with the guts of a Gerry Byrne are always useful in a side which aspires to winning a big competition. That Gerry was not called upon to play in any of the World Cup games is immaterial.

Then there was Big Jack Charlton, just twenty-nine and the possessor of sixteen England caps at the time of the World Cup. When he finished his playing career he had collected

thirty-five and also made a record number of 629 appearances for Leeds United. He was, and is, a remarkable man
and I love the quote he gave to 'Kicking and Screaming':

> I was having a pint on a Saturday night after I'd played
> in London and we were meeting on the Sunday for the
> game on Wednesday, and I stood at the bar and Alf
> came in and we were talking at the bar.
>   I said to him, 'Why did you pick me, Alf?' He said,
> 'Well, Jack, I've watched you play. You're very good in
> the air, you're quite mobile, you're a good tackler, and I
> know you won't trust Bobby Moore.' I said, 'What do
> you mean?' And Alf said, 'What I'm trying to say is if
> Gordon Banks gives the ball to you as a central
> defender, you'll give it back to Gordon and say kick it,
> but if you give the ball to Bobby Moore, Bobby will join
> in the build-up in midfield, through to the forwards,
> and if he makes a mistake at any stage I know, because
> I've watched you play, that you will always go across
> and play behind him and allow him to make the mis-
> take.'

Even during his playing career, Jack was a real country gent.
He loves fishing and shooting. But he also loves football and
he was an outstanding manager at Middlesbrough, Sheffield
Wednesday and Newcastle United, before taking over the
Republic of Ireland side and transforming it from perpetual
losers into frequent winners. Mick McCarthy, who has succeeded Big Jack as manager, will have a hard act to follow.

George Cohen was twenty-six when he played in the World
Cup, ten years after he had made his début for Fulham at the
tender age of sixteen. It took him just eighteen months to

establish himself as a regular first-teamer at Craven Cottage and, like Jimmy Armfield, Jack and Bobby Charlton, Roger Hunt and Geoff Hurst, he was a one-club man.

He had to retire in 1969 with a serious knee injury, but a much more bitter blow hit him in the following year. He was diagnosed as having cancer.

George had a family to support and a thriving property development company to help him do it. After an operation he gradually got back to work, but he suffered two relapses, one in 1978 and another in 1980.

His fight against cancer in the 1980s coincided with the collapse of the property market, so trouble was piled on to trouble. But, as George explains philosophically, 'worse things can happen than the property market going bad'. The strain on his family almost equalled the strain on himself. 'In fact I think it's much worse for the family,' he told me.

As he struggled with his persistent illness he never forgot that others too faced disaster and death. When the dreadful fire at Bradford in 1985 claimed so many lives it was decided to put on a 'replay' of the 1966 World Cup Final between England and West Germany at Elland Road, Leeds to raise funds for the victims' families. On 28 July, George Cohen insisted on starting the game with his former England colleagues. He was substituted after a few minutes, but it was a brave effort for such a severely ill man to turn out at all. But that is George Cohen. The story has a happy ending because, in January 1990, he was discharged from the Royal Marsden Hospital with a clean bill of health. Long may he go on, fit and well, to enjoy all the good fortune he deserves.

Ron Flowers was the father of the squad at the age of thirty-one. He had never expected to be chosen for the final twenty-two. He had only played in the England side once in the last twelve months and believed his international career was over.

Over it was indeed, for although he was in the squad, he never got a game during the World Cup so he was left 'stranded' on forty-nine caps in his illustrious career. He played one more season for Wolves before retiring to concentrate on his sports shop ... and golf. He has now retired from the shop and left it in the capable hands of his son, but the golf is still going well.

He was once a very low handicap player – even today he plays off eight – and was so keen on the game that he often caddied at professional tournaments. The caddying days are over, but he is seen more often playing on the golf course than he is watching football. He does sometimes go along to watch Wolves in their splendid new stadium and is full of praise for the way Jack Hayward, the club's Chairman, treats the former players. Mr Hayward has told them all, he says, 'Whenever you want to come there's always a seat for you, and a drink.'

Norman Hunter was another defender who got into the squad but was never called upon to play. Norman was only twenty-two in 1966, by which time he had been capped four times, but he went on to play for England until 1975 and finished up with twenty-eight caps. After he retired as a player he tried his luck as a manager, but now he concentrates on the business he runs with his wife and on the commentating he does for Radio Leeds on the Leeds United games.

Robert Frederick Chelsea Moore was born on 2 April 1941 at Barking, in Essex. He made his league début for West Ham United on 8 September 1958 and in sixteen years with the Hammers he made 642 appearances and scored twenty-six goals. He led West Ham to an FA Cup victory over Preston North End in 1964 and to victory in the European Cup Winners' Cup the following season when West Ham beat Munich 1860 in a Final which received a special award for sportsmanship.

In 1974 he joined Fulham and in 1975 was the captain of the Fulham side beaten in the FA Cup Final 2–0 – by West Ham United! In three years with Fulham, Moore played 150 times but scored just one goal.

His international career, which began in Peru on 20 May 1962, spanned eleven years, during which time he won 108 caps, a record 90 of them as captain. He was also selected eight times for the England Under-23 team, represented the Football League twelve times and won a record number of England Youth caps – eighteen.

Bobby was Footballer of the Year in both 1963 and 1964, and in 1967 was awarded the Order of the British Empire.

Ray Wilson went into the World Cup at the age of thirty-one and with 445 caps to his credit. His international career continued after the World Cup win, which isn't surprising as Alf Ramsey classed him as the best left back he had ever seen.

Ray had played for England in the third and fourth place decider in the 1968 European Championships, but at the beginning of the following season a severe knee injury all but ended his career. He did give good service to Oldham Athletic, whom he joined from Everton, and then went on to Bradford City, but he was sensible enough to know he could go on no longer.

So it was on to a new career. His father-in-law was a funeral director and Ray joined him in the business. As he put it, 'It's not a glamorous occupation, but when the country went into recession I realized how lucky I was because the undertaking business never knows recession!'

The Wilsons now live in a farmhouse on a smallholding between Huddersfield and Halifax and they love it. 'The countryside where I live is pretty wild,' admits Ray, 'but it's lovely country and I love walking over it. I sometimes walk for six or seven hours at a time and sometimes I go walking in the Lake District, which is just as magnificent.'

Come the World Cup, Alan Ball was only twenty and had played for England ten times, which proved that Alf Ramsey was a man of his word. When he had selected Alan for his first international he had told him, 'That's the first of ten caps you will get for England and by that time we will know just how good you are.'

Bally was born in Farnworth on the outskirts of Bolton and went to Farnworth Grammar School. So did I, but nobody thought of putting a plaque on the school wall to com-memorate the fact. Instead they pulled the school down! That was hardly the proper way to honour a footballer who played for Blackpool, Everton and Arsenal and seventy-two times for England.

He finished his playing career with Southampton at the ripe old age of thirty-eight. Then it was straight into manage-ment, with Portsmouth, Stoke City and Southampton, but perhaps his most successful stint was at lowly Exeter City, where he did the job he loves best and does so well – coach-ing the youngsters.

Eventually he got the call from his old pal, Francis Lee, the Chairman of Manchester City. They were partners in the 1970 World Cup squad so it was natural that the two Lancastrians should team up to try to restore Manchester City to its former glory. And if that fails, these two racing enthusiasts can always argue about the form of the horses, especially those trained by Francis Lee.

Ian Callaghan, the Liverpool winger, with one cap under his belt (or wherever players keep their international caps!) got one game, against France, in the 1966 competition and two matches after the World Cup. It didn't seem a just reward for a fine, aggressive wingman.

He is now a busy man in his retirement. He owns two public houses in partnership with his old Liverpool colleague, Geoff Strong, plays a lot of golf (and plays it well) and is the chairman of the Littlewoods 'Spot the Ball' committee. Littlewoods have hospitality boxes at both Anfield and Goodison Park, so Ian Callaghan is often a guest of theirs, but he admits to being a bad watcher. Most ex-players are.

Bobby Charlton, described by Jim Armfield as 'the ace in our pack' at the 1966 World Cup, still had a lot of playing time left in him after the 1966 triumph. He was part of the 1970 squad, and his last international was against West Germany in that year's quarter-final. Sadly he was substituted in the match, which England lost 3–2, so he won't remember his one hundred and sixth and final appearance for England with any relish. Nevertheless, he can look back on the fact that he still holds the goal-scoring record for England – forty-nine goals in his 106 internationals.

But back in February 1958 we wondered whether his career had ended with the Munich air disaster which killed so many of his team-mates, Manchester United officials and sports journalists.

In those days Bobby was not a regular first-team player at Old Trafford, but as soon as he recovered from his injuries he was flung into the fray and immediately shot to stardom.

His impact on the game was so sensational that two months after he was rescued from the wrecked aircraft in Munich he was chosen to play for England against Scotland at Hampden Park, and celebrated his first international with a cracking goal. He was a member of the party which went on a pre-World Cup tour, and he scored both goals in a 2–1 win over Portugal.

The second match of the tour was against Yugoslavia in Belgrade, on the ground where Manchester United had played a European Cup tie just before their ill-fated flight home. Charlton was chosen to play, no doubt in the hope that it would help to exorcise some of his memories (rather on the same lines that show jumpers are told to remount after a fall, and attempt to jump the same fence again). But plane crashes are somewhat different from falling off a horse, and Charlton didn't do himself justice in Belgrade, where England were thrashed 5–0.

Charlton was left out of the side for the third game in Moscow, but he was chosen for the World Cup squad. He was not, however, picked for any of the first-round matches, all of which ended in draws, against the Soviet Union, Brazil (without Pelé) and Austria. The media began a campaign for the return of Charlton for the play-off against the Soviet Union for a place in the quarter-final, but the pleas fell on deaf ears and England, without Bobby Charlton, were beaten by the only goal of the match.

Newspaper headlines demanded to know why Charlton was not selected and Walter Winterbottom was bombarded with that question at all his press conferences and, in fact, wherever he went. He tells a lovely story against himself about the Charlton incident. After his return home he visited his son's school and told the headmaster how he had been greeted by his family at Heathrow Airport:

As I came out of the door from the Customs area I saw my wife, my daughter and my son. I kissed my wife and daughter and they both said, 'Welcome home.' I noticed my son was looking downcast and I thought he was a little put off by all the kissing. So I went up to him, held out my hand and said, 'Hello, son.' He didn't take my hand. He just looked me straight in the eye and demanded, 'Why didn't you choose Bobby Charlton?'

I must admit to being staggered when my son asked me the same question everyone I had met had asked me.

The headmaster looked at me, paused for a moment as if trying to think of the right reply and then said, 'Well, why DIDN'T you choose Bobby Charlton?'

Bobby became a fixture in the England side for the next twelve years, so nobody ever had to ask, 'Why didn't you choose Bobby Charlton?' again.

After the end of his glittering playing career Charlton went into management with Preston North End. But, like many other great players, he didn't turn out to be a great manager.

Now fifty-eight, he is still putting a lot back into the game he served so well. He is a director of Manchester United, is frequently called upon to do high-calibre sports promotions and runs coaching schools, both at home and abroad. His name continues to be a byword wherever football is played. I remember being with Manchester United when they played Sarajevo in one of the European competitions and Bobby Charlton's picture was on all the tickets. Off the field he is a keen worker for charity and plays golf with the same enthusiasm and will to win as he played football.

One of the three recognized wingmen in the 1966 squad was John Connelly, who began his career with Burnley and was then transferred to Manchester United. One thing worried him: the fact that few people pronounced his name correctly. Most people called him either 'Connolly' or 'CONely'. The correct pronunciation, John told me early in his career, was 'Con-NELLY'. I received many letters from viewers asking me, 'Why do you pronounce that outside right's name in such a funny way?' and it got almost as boring as, 'Why didn't you choose ...' But we won't go into that again.

John played as an orthodox outside right in the first match against Uruguay and felt he was in good form and that the 4–3–3 system suited him. But that game, his twentieth appearance for England, proved to be his last.

It certainly wasn't the last first-class football saw of him, though, because he went on playing until 1974, by which time he had made 565 appearances and scored 179 goals for his clubs – Burnley, Manchester United, Blackburn Rovers and Bury.

A Lancastrian through and through, and an East Lancastrian at that, it is only natural that he should have settled down in Nelson, where he runs a fish-and-chip shop by the name of Connelly's Plaice. He told me:

> We have a regular clientele, but many of them are real friends rather than just customers. Sometimes we chat about the old days and the games of the past, but some of the younger folk don't really know that I was an international footballer who was in the World Cup winning squad and who played alongside people like Best, Charlton and Law. But that doesn't worry me. You can't expect to live on your memories for ever.
>
> These days I don't go and watch much football. It's not that I have anything against the game, but it's difficult to find the time. Anyway, like so many players of my era, I just wanted to play. I was never a good watcher.

I've recently taken up golf, but I'm not much good at it. What I really like, and so does my wife, is walking. We often walk five or six miles in the dales or in the Lake District. One of these days we'll probably walk east over the dales and maybe we'll bump into Ray Wilson. That would be good fun.

Like John Connelly's, George Eastham's international career came to a halt with the 1966 World Cup. He was a member of the squad, but didn't get a game so didn't add to his total of nineteen caps. However, that is eighteen more than his father, also called George Eastham, also slightly built and also an excellent ball player, won before the Second World War.

George now lives in South Africa, in good health following a hip operation.

Another resident in South Africa is Terry Paine, the Southampton winger who did something Eastham didn't do. He got a game in the 1966 World Cup, playing in the 2–0 victory over Mexico. It was his nineteenth cap for England and it brought him level with Eastham. But there were to be no more.

Martin Peters was an international beginner at the start of the World Cup with just three England appearances to his name. But Alf Ramsey had made public his view that the then young (twenty-two years of age) West Ham United midfielder was ten years ahead of his time. Once again Alf was proved right. Peters' international career continued until 1974, four years after he joined Tottenham Hotspur.

Peters – nicknamed 'The Duke' by Norman Hunter because of his tall, lean resemblance to the Duke of

Edinburgh – played sixty-seven times for England. After his retirement he tried his hand at managing Sheffield United but that was not the success he hoped it would be. He is now a successful businessman with the same motor insurance group for which Geoff Hurst works.

It is an exacting job, calling for a great deal of travelling, but Martin still finds time to turn up at every Tottenham Hotspur's home match, where he helps on the commercial side, entertaining the sponsors and guests in the various lounges at White Hart Lane.

Perhaps the greatest character in the 1966 World Cup squad was Norbert Peter Stiles. Only knee-high to a grasshopper, he was one of the most enthusiastic, non-stop players in the game. Though he always played with a grin on his face, he was a ferocious tackler, sometimes even called dirty. He was at pains to point out that he was only small, he had no teeth (his toothless grin when he left his false teeth in the dressing-room was his trade mark) and his eyesight was atrocious, so how could he be successful in a rough and tumble? But successful he was.

When he joined Manchester United as a junior he had to resort to subterfuge to get his chance to become a star player. He never wore his glasses when he went to the club, and his colleagues suddenly discovered during a card-playing session one day that Nobby, as Norbert Peter was universally known, just could not see. He pleaded with them not to give the game away and they didn't. Nobby played in contact lenses and it is still a joke at Old Trafford that they took on an almost blind youngster who then became an international star.

In one match on which I commentated, the contact lenses worked against Nobby. Manchester United were playing

Estudiantes de la Plata in the 1968 Intercontinental Cup Final, in the fearsome Boca Juniors Stadium in Buenos Aires, Argentina.

The South American press found out about the contact lenses and it was splashed all over the newspapers that if they were knocked out of his eyes, Nobby Stiles couldn't see. From the kick-off that was the plan of the Estudiantes players and they succeeded. It wasn't long before we had the bizarre sight of Nobby on his knees feeling the pitch to try to find the lenses which had been dislodged!

United's strategy in that match was for Nobby to keep breaking through the middle, where he wasn't handled with kid gloves by the Argentine defenders, none of whom was penalized. On one of Nobby's breaks he was given offside and raised an arm in disbelief. He was immediately sent off. On the long walk round the touchline to the dressing-rooms at one end of the pitch he was pelted with all sorts of rubbish, but nothing could stop that jaunty walk or wipe the smile off his face. The next day he went shopping in the heart of the city and was fêted by the locals, who wanted to shake his hand!

Stiles finished his international career in 1970 with twenty-eight caps and retired from playing four years later after spells with Middlesbrough and Preston North End, where Bobby Charlton was manager at the time. When Bobby left, Nobby took over the reins, but he was sacked when North End were relegated.

He joined West Bromwich Albion as caretaker manager and then became youth team coach, but his great joy was going back to Manchester United to look after 'the kids' as he called them. He did such a good job that they brought honours to the club, and at Manchester United today they know they owe a debt to Nobby Stiles for his work with his youngsters who have now become stars.

He is now retired but spends a lot of time entertaining guests with his witty speeches at sportsmen's dinners.

Now for the three strikers – Greaves, Hunt and Hurst. The Greaves story comes later, but, to clean up a common misconception here, many people still think that when Greaves was injured in 1966 against France it was Roger Hunt who took his place. Nothing of the sort. Hunt was an established member of the international side: it was Geoff Hurst who stepped in for Greaves, and stepped in so magnificently.

Roger Hunt had played thirteen internationals by the time the 1966 World Cup began and he finished his international career in 1969 with thirty-four caps. At one time he and Greaves vied for the same position. As Roger puts it:

> Greaves was a great player. He was England's leading scorer until Bobby Charlton took over from him. I used to get into the side when Jimmy was injured or when he was on European duty with Tottenham. Then Jimmy was struck down with jaundice and I got a regular place in the team. In the World Cup we were the two strikers in all the three first-round matches. It was when Jimmy was injured against France that Geoff Hurst took over.

Roger was a great club player for Liverpool. He was their leading scorer of all time with 245 goals to his credit until Ian Rush broke the record during the 1995–96 season, much to the dismay of Ian's father, who was a great fan of Hunt's. In fact, it was Mr Rush who used to refer to Roger as Sir Roger Hunt, which is how he is still known to many Liverpool fans.

Towards the end of his career he was transferred to Bolton Wanderers and became as popular at Burnden Park as he had been at Anfield. Today he has divided loyalties. He goes to watch both Liverpool and Bolton and says, 'Both clubs have a very special place in my heart.'

When he finished playing, Roger joined Hunt Brothers, the family firm of haulage contractors founded by his father and uncle in the 1930s. In the summer of 1995 Roger decided to retire and spend more of his time on the golf course. He is also a member of the Pools Panel and, like so many other ex-pros, does a lot of after-dinner speaking.

Lancashire-born Geoff Hurst was a latecomer to the England scene. It was only in 1966 that he won the first of his forty-nine caps, and it came as a great surprise to him when he broke through into the eleven for the quarter-final game against Argentina. But once he got into the team, Hurst was on the winning side in the three World Cup matches he played. In those three games England scored seven goals, and Geoff got four of them.

After giving super service to West Ham United, Hurst had spells with Stoke City and West Bromwich Albion before taking over at Chelsea as manager in 1979. He lasted just two years – one year longer than Danny Blanchflower! – and thinks that being a football manager is daft. But then Chelsea has long been known as the graveyard of managers!

Perhaps the best assessment of Geoff Hurst the player came from Jimmy Armfield:

We were lucky to be able to call on Geoff Hurst. He had two good feet, he was good in the air and he would run all day for you. He was a very good technical player. He wasn't just a good player, he was a great player.

In fact I rate him as the best and most complete centre forward England has ever had.

There is nothing I can add to that, except to say, 'Thanks, Geoff, for scoring that fourth goal in the one hundred and twentieth minute on 30 July 1966 and giving me the chance to say ... what I did.'

Having extricated himself from the minefield of football club management, Geoff Hurst joined a motor insurance company and is now a manager with its parent company.

And still doing a great double act with Martin Peters.

5

The Jimmy Greaves Saga

Reams and reams have been written about Jimmy Greaves and the 1966 World Cup. Some of it is true; much of it isn't. One thing, though, is certain: if you ask Greavsie, who always has been and still is a most approachable fellow, he will gladly tell you the truth, the whole truth and nothing but the truth.

Before I start telling the Jimmy Greaves saga, let me state that there is no animosity between Greaves and Alf Ramsey, nor has there ever been.

But let's go back to the beginning of the story, the story of an East Ham boy, who was born on 20 February 1940, just in time for the blitz, an East Ham boy destined to become a world football star.

He played for his school team and was chosen to represent Dagenham Boys and Essex Boys. (Another youngster, born twenty years before Greaves, also represented Dagenham Boys and Essex Boys. His name was Alfred Ernest Ramsey!)

Unlike Alf Ramsey, Greaves also played for London Boys, and as he was an avid Tottenham Hotspur supporter, everyone was convinced that he was a certainty to join Spurs when he was old enough. But during the 1954–55 season, when Greaves was supposed to be heading for White Hart Lane, the Spurs manager, Arthur Rowe, the architect of the great push-and-run team, fell ill. Before his successor, Jimmy Anderson, had settled into his job, Greaves, then the hottest young property around, was persuaded to forget North London and go west, young man, to Chelsea, where he joined a number of other East London boys on the Chelsea junior staff. Among his new colleagues were Les Allen and Terry Venables, both of whom, like Greaves, were eventually to join Tottenham.

Greaves made a sensational impact on Chelsea as a junior. He was selected for Middlesex Boys and then for the England Youth side. That is where I first met up with him.

The BBC received permission to televise live from Upton Park the Youth International between England and Luxembourg on Saturday evening, 2 February 1957. I had heard a lot about the young Chelsea star who scored goals as easily as some people shell peas, so it was an exciting prospect to be able to go along and see for myself what the young lad could do. And there were other soon-to-be-familiar names in the England side that evening: David Gaskell (Manchester United); David Wright (Barnsley Grammar School), captain, John Sanchez (Arsenal); Eddie Colton (Sheffield Wednesday), Colin Holmes (Southampton), John Lyall (West Ham United); Mike Connolly (Doncaster Rovers), Jimmy Greaves (Chelsea), Barry Bridges (Chelsea), John Cartwright (West Ham United), Reg Stratton (Woking). I know that Luxembourg is not one of the leading footballing nations, but, even allowing for that, the performance of the England team (all of whom had to be under eighteen on 1 September 1956) was amazing. They lost an early goal but then ran out winners by 7–1. Jimmy Greaves equalized in the sixth minute and so began his remarkable record of always scoring on his début. Altogether he scored four of the seven goals, the other three coming from Bridges (2) and Stratton. On top of that, Greaves shot well over the bar from a penalty kick!

Exactly a month later, the England Youth team had another home match, this time against Holland at Griffin Park, the home of Brentford Football Club. Again England had a bad start and were 3–0 down after only thirty-five minutes.

Then came the Greaves-led counter attack. Five minutes before half-time, Dodson, of Arsenal, scored, and this was followed by two goals within a minute, both scored by Greaves. England were level at 3–3.

Holland scored again in the first minute of the second half, and this was too much for Greaves. Twice more he scored and for the first time in the game England were in the lead, by five goals to four. Although Holland equalized to make the final score 5–5, I had seen enough of Chelsea's young wonder to convince me that England had a new star on their hands. He had scored eight of England's twelve goals in those two internationals, and by the time he signed apprentice professional forms for Chelsea in May 1957 he had scored 114 goals for Chelsea Juniors.

On 24 August 1957 he made his début for the Chelsea First Division side in a local derby against Tottenham Hotspur at White Hart Lane. The game ended in a one-all draw, and Jimmy Greaves kept up the tradition of scoring on his début. He played half a dozen games for Chelsea before winning his first Under-23 cap against Bulgaria at the Chelsea ground. On his Under-23 début he scored not once, but twice!

His reputation as a goal scorer spread to Italy and Chelsea agreed a transfer with AC Milan at the end of the 1960–61 season. By that time, in his three full seasons for Chelsea Jimmy Greaves had scored 129 goals.

I was doing the commentary once when he scored five against Wolverhampton Wanderers, whose defence was marshalled by the great Billy Wright. And thereby hangs a tale.

Choosing teams has always been one of the favourite and most harmless pastimes of football fans the world over. It doesn't matter whether it's your local team you choose or whether you project yourself into the big time and pick an England – or Scottish, Welsh or Irish – side. With England due to play Russia at Wembley on 22 October 1958, Ronnie Noble, who was Paul Fox's right-hand man on the old *Sportsview* programme, believed it would make a good, controversial item for the programme if he and I picked a team and suggested that this was the team that should play Russia. We realized it would have to be controversial otherwise the item would be a damp squib.

Since the two main fixtures in the England side of the day were Billy Wright and Johnny Haynes, we decided that one or both should go. Ronnie and I wracked what brains we had between us but neither of us could come up with a credible alternative to Billy Wright. So it was Johnny Haynes who had to go. But for whom? We both then remembered the five goals Jimmy Greaves had scored against Wolves – and we had the film to prove it.

That was it then: it was Jimmy Greaves in, Johnny Haynes out. We were throwing the goalscoring sensation of the season in against the powerful Russians.

As we knew it would, the item, which lasted less than two minutes, created a stir. Just what we wanted.

Then came the game at Wembley. It was nip and tuck all the way but England ended up winning 5–0. And who scored the goals? Nat Lofthouse, Bobby Charlton from a penalty and … Johnny Haynes got a hat-trick!

The following Wednesday I appeared on *Sportsview*
dressed in sackcloth, and who should be in the studio that
night helping out with an item about tiddlywinks – yes,
tiddlywinks? Spike Milligan. As the cameras showed a con-
trite Wolstenholme, Spike Milligan appeared and sprinkled
ashes all over me! It was completely spontaneous and unre-
hearsed, because Spike, mischievous as ever, had thought it
up himself and told nobody.

Although the England team manager didn't take my
advice for the game against Russia, Greaves was included in
the party for the close-season tour. And what a tour it was!
After a Wembley date with Italy on 6 May 1959 – that ended
all square at 2–2 – we set off for matches against Brazil in
Rio's Maracaná Stadium, Peru in Lima, Mexico (in the
University Stadium not the Aztec) in Mexico City, and finally
against the United States of America in Los Angeles.

Nobody was surprised when we lost 2–0 to Brazil, but it
was a bit of a shock to go down to Peru 4–1. Everything
seemed to be in England's favour. The Peruvian side was not
highly rated, there was no climatic problem, the stadium was
beautiful and the pitch was the sort of pitch most clubs in
England would love to have. But England were outclassed.
They were two down at half-time, and Seminario scored a
hat-trick in Peru's comfortable win. The England goal was
scored by the nineteen-year-old Jimmy Greaves, who was
making his international début, and thus kept up his remarkable record of scoring on his début at each level of the
game.

Lima was a fascinating city, situated on the coast against
the distant backdrop of the mighty Andes. Peru was under
Martial Law at the time, but nothing interfered with us as we
bought our llama skin rugs and drank our pisco sours.

Which was how, while having a drink with the late Jack

Wood, then with the *Daily Mail*, we somehow got caught up in a wedding reception and ended up being treated as members of the family and being invited by the bride's father, who was Mayor of one of Lima's suburbs, to a reception in the Mayor's Parlour.

From Lima to Mexico City, a huge city built on a swamp, which would possibly win the pollution stakes in a photo-finish from Tokyo and Rio de Janeiro. It was steamingly hot, and at Mexico City's altitude the sun can be pretty dangerous, as one of the English team found out. He spent a few minutes sunbathing on the roof of the hotel and got painfully burned. Nevertheless, he turned out for what proved to be England's third straight defeat.

We have to remember that the kick-off was at midday, we were 8,000 feet above sea level and the temperature was in the nineties – not really ideal conditions for English footballers. We had the advantage of taking the lead after sixteen minutes but the Mexicans were not long in equalizing, and soon after the restart they scored the goal that won the match. While all this was going on, there was a slight earth tremor, causing the press seats at the top of the stand to wobble frighteningly, but the television positions were lower down and we felt nothing at all.

It wasn't the brightest of England performances although Greaves seemed to get better with every game he played. But, while he looked totally at home on the pitch, off the field he seemed a little boy lost. It was his first tour and he hadn't yet got into the swing of things.

One evening when three of us were going out for dinner we saw Jimmy sitting alone in the hotel foyer and invited him to join us.

We went to a restaurant called the Catacombs, where the waiters play jokes on the customers, such as dangling a toy spider on a strand of elastic in front of your face. Jimmy almost leapt out of his skin but then saw the funny side of it.

It was a rather downcast England party that boarded the aircraft at Mexico City bound for Los Angeles, where the 'welcome' in Immigration did little to bring sunshine into our lives. Most of us media characters had the same question flung at us: 'Why have you got so many Commie visas?', and had to explain we travelled to Eastern European countries to cover sporting events. The whole rigmarole got so tedious, as the Immigration Officer brought out a book which listed the names of people to be denied entry, that one of our party suggested, 'Why don't you have a book listing those who are welcome in the United States; it wouldn't have to be so large.' That did little to break the ice.

However, there was one moment of light relief. The late Joe Mears, then the Chairman of the Football Association, was, of course, the leading member of the party and he was asked the usual question by the Immigration Officer, 'What is the purpose of your visit to the United States?' Joe tried to keep it simple by replying, 'I am the Chairman with the England football team.'

The Immigration Officer looked puzzled. 'The England football team? I didn't know you played football in England,' he said in sheer disbelief.

Nobody was in the mood to explain that we played football, the world game, and not football, the exclusively American game.

When we were eventually allowed in, we received superb hospitality. The sports commentators of Los Angeles organized a splendid lunch in honour of the English press and television visitors, during which I had the pleasure of meeting Jack Kramer, the former tennis champion.

The game itself was a bit of a farce. Played at the 22,000-capacity Wrigley Field, it had the makings of a sensation. The Americans could have been three up before we were half-way through the first forty-five minutes. They scored in the nineteenth minute, and a few minutes later had the ball in the net again. This time, however, the 'goal' was disallowed for offside. We had hardly got over the shock when Don Howe made a careless back pass well wide of Eddie Hopkinson, the English goalkeeper. Hopkinson scampered across his goal and managed to grab the ball, but many people thought the ball had already crossed the line. Ray Morgan, the Canadian referee, didn't agree.

England were finding the going tough because Wrigley Field was a baseball stadium, and the half England were attacking had the baseball diamond gouged out of the lush turf. The combination of grass and dirt made it impossible to play good football, and at half-time it was a goal each, Bradley having scored for England.

The second half was, as the Americans say, a whole new ball game. Attacking the half which was totally grassed over, England found it easy and scored at will. Charlton – Bobby, that is – scored a hat-trick, Flowers got two and Kevan and Haynes one each. So the tour at least ended with a win.

But back to Jimmy Greaves. With his goal tally standing at 129 league and cup goals for Chelsea, eleven goals in eleven games for the England Under-23 team, one goal in four appearances for the Football League, two for Young England in a game against England, and an incredible fifteen goals in fifteen full internationals, he joined AC Milan in June 1961.

Greaves continued his goal-scoring form in the Italian League with nine goals in fourteen games for Milan and he could have been a sensation in Italy, but Jimmy and Italy didn't get on too well. Not able to speak the language and straining against the strict club discipline, within six months Greaves let it be known that he would like to return home. Many fine players from the United Kingdom have tried their luck in Italy and been a success: John Charles, Eddie Firmani, Ray Wilkins, David Platt, Joe Jordan, Liam Brady. What they had in common was that they all spoke Italian. The players who failed to stay the course – Greaves, Denis Law, Joe Baker, Ian Rush – also had a common denominator: they didn't speak the language.

Milan did nothing to deter him and, in December 1961, Greaves signed for Tottenham Hotspur. The club was still on a high after completing the League and Cup double and Greaves decided he would show them that he hadn't lost that début-scoring record. He scored not one, not two, but three against Blackpool in his first match for Spurs.

Greaves was a huge success at White Hart Lane until he went to West Ham United in 1970 as part of the deal that saw Martin Peters on his way to Tottenham. And what a record Greaves left behind at Spurs! In the 1962–63 season he scored thirty-seven goals in the old First Division – still a club record. In league matches he scored 220 goals – still a club record – in 322 appearances.

Add to that thirty-two goals in thirty-six FA Cup ties, five in eight Football League Cup ties, nine in fourteen European games, and forty goals in forty other matches, making a grand total of 306 goals in 420 games. How's that for a strike rate?

He didn't disappoint the West Ham fans on his début: he scored twice to keep up his amazing record. He only played thirty-eight games for the Hammers before he retired at the end of the 1970–71 season. In those thirty-eight games he produced thirteen goals.

Before his retirement he had his eyes on a place in England's World Cup team and, despite a nasty bout of jaundice, he recovered sufficiently not only to make the squad but to be in the team for the first three games. It was in the third of these, against France, that he suffered the nasty shin injury which cost him his chance of playing in the Final.

After the victory against Portugal in the semi-final, with England now through to the Final, Alf Ramsey had a selection problem. Should he keep his winning team or should he bring in the now fully fit, Greaves, a goalscorer *par excellence*? The decision to keep Hurst, who had scored the only goal against Argentina and then played very well against Portugal, was Alf Ramsey's and no one else's. Greaves was, therefore, out.

Many stories have since been told of how the decision was made, some even suggesting that there was some dark mystery about the final selection, but there wasn't. Alf simply made his mind up and was willing to stand or fall by the team he had chosen.

There were fierce arguments on the day of the Final as to whether Alf had made the right decision or not. There were no fierce arguments after the match!

In the ensuing years many people have continued to say that Greaves should have played in the Final. They are the same people who claim that Greaves has never forgiven Ramsey and that the pair haven't spoken to each other since 1966. Furthermore, it is widely believed that Jimmy Greaves has been carrying an outsized chip on his shoulder these last thirty years, and that his omission from the World Cup Final team was responsible for his 'subsequent loss of form'.

What subsequent loss of form? After the World Cup Greaves continued to score goals for Spurs and then for West Ham United, and the following season he played for England

against Scotland at Wembley on 15 April 1967 when Scotland
won by three goals to two (and thereby won the right to call
themselves World Champions ... according to the Scots, that
is!), against Spain at Wembley on 24 May 1967 and three
days later against Austria in Vienna. Both those games were
won, two goals to nil against Spain and by the only goal of
the match against Austria.

It was only then that Greaves' international career ended,
with the superb record of forty-four goals in fifty-seven international matches.

What about the outsized chip on the shoulder and the
silence between Greaves and Ramsey? Let Jimmy speak for
himself. This is what he told me:

Alf and I have always got on. He is as good as gold and
it is nonsense to say we never speak to each other. In
fact all the stories about me and the World Cup are nonsense. The controversy about whether I should have
played in the Final or not seems to bother the media and
the fans more than it bothers me. I have had too many
battles to fight in my life than to keep worrying about
playing in this match or that match.

Of course I was disappointed. Of course I was upset.
Who wouldn't be, for goodness sake? To play for your
country in the Final of the World Cup is the pinnacle of
anyone's career and I missed it. But only eleven
Englishmen could make it on the day, and if you want to
know whether they did a good job or not, look in the
record books.

When the World Cup was over I went on holiday for
ten days and then had to join Spurs on a pre-season tour,
so I had a job to do. But looking back on my disappointment, perhaps I should have cried my eyes out seeing

what happened to Gazza when he cried just because he'd got himself suspended and wouldn't have been able to play in the Final if England got there – which they didn't.

Looking back on it all makes me realize that it was just part of life, and I wish that missing out on the Final was the only thing that had gone wrong with my life.

The true facts are that I got a bad gash on my leg against France and it puffed up. There was no way I could have been fit to play against Argentina, and when Geoff (Hurst) came in and scored against Argentina, I knew I wouldn't play in the Final. Alf would obviously keep the same team against Portugal, and if we won that one there was no way that he would contemplate a change other than for an injury.

What I would liked to have done is not to have hung around when I was injured. I turned out in a friendly we had against Arsenal at London Colney three days before the Final, and I only just got through that. So when Alf told me on the big day that I wasn't in the team it was only confirmation of what I already knew.

It is silly to keep bringing the whole thing up. It has never been a big issue with me and it wasn't a shock when I was left out of the side. I am only sorry I picked up the injury, but that sort of thing has happened before and it will happen again.

People should remember that Alf Ramsey was a great manager and he did a great job for England. He was single-minded and you need a man like that running your national side. There is no animosity between him and me. There never has been and never will be. I admire the way he did his job.

And Jim, we admire the way you did yours.

6

On Your Marks ... Get Set ...

The squad of twenty-two players had been selected. The other finalists, all fifteen of them, had arrived and knew where and whom they would be playing. It was a case of 'On your marks ... Get set ...' and waiting for the 'Go' after the Opening Ceremony and the first game, between England and Uruguay, at Wembley on Monday evening, 11 July 1966.

The draw took place on Thursday, 1 January at The Royal Lancaster Hotel, London, which served as headquarters for FIFA and the press throughout the competition.

It is difficult to arrange a World Cup draw to satisfy everyone (when I use the word 'arrange' I obviously don't mean it in the 'fix' context). It would be foolish to put all the sixteen teams into the hat and draw them willy-nilly. There has to be some seeding, and it would not be popular if, say, all the South Americans were drawn in one group, thereby making sure two of them would be eliminated in the first round.

What happened in 1966 was that the sixteen finalists were split into four groups and then one nation from each group would be drawn into each playing area. The areas were

London (Wembley and White City), Midlands (Villa Park and Hillsborough), the North West (Goodison Park and Old Trafford) and the North East (Ayresome Park and Roker Park).

The four groups were arranged as South America (Argentina, Brazil, Chile and Uruguay); Latin nations (France, Italy, Portugal and Spain); Europe (England, Hungary, West Germany and Russia); and 'the others' (Bulgaria, Mexico, North Korea and Switzerland).

The draw was televised in the early evening, but the South American radio stations couldn't wait for the rest of the world. They began transmitting something like two hours before anyone else. It was strange to sit at the position allocated to the BBC and listen to the South Americans working themselves into a frenzy. I had seen and heard them before and knew what they were like, how they seem to press a button that releases all the passion they feel about the game. But to the hotel staff and people who had never been to South America, it was fascinating to see men waving their arms and screaming their heads off when absolutely nothing was happening. South American tonsils must be the toughest in the world!

When the draw got under way, the non-seeded nations came out of the drum and were added to the seeded nations in four groups:

GROUP ONE

July 11	England	v	Uruguay at Wembley
July 13	France	v	Mexico at Wembley
July 15	Uruguay	v	France at the White City
July 16	Mexico	v	England at Wembley
July 19	Mexico	v	Uruguay at Wembley
July 20	France	v	England at Wembley

GROUP TWO

July 12	West Germany	*v*	Switzerland at Hillsborough
July 13	Spain	*v*	Argentina at Villa Park
July 15	Switzerland	*v*	Spain at Hillsborough
July 16	Argentina	*v*	West Germany at Villa Park
July 19	Argentina	*v*	Switzerland at Hillsborough
July 20	Spain	*v*	West Germany at Villa Park

GROUP THREE

July 12	Brazil	*v*	Bulgaria at Goodison Park
July 13	Portugal	*v*	Hungary at Old Trafford
July 15	Hungary	*v*	Brazil at Goodison Park
July 16	Portugal	*v*	Bulgaria at Old Trafford
July 19	Portugal	*v*	Brazil at Goodison Park
July 20	Hungary	*v*	Bulgaria at Old Trafford

GROUP FOUR

July 12	Russia	*v*	North Korea at Ayresome Park
July 13	Italy	*v*	Chile at Roker Park
July 15	North Korea	*v*	Chile at Ayresome Park
July 16	Russia	*v*	Italy at Roker Park
July 19	Italy	*v*	North Korea at Ayresome Park
July 20	Russia	*v*	Chile at Roker Park

The draw completed, the hubbub subsided and the South American commentators reached for their gargles and throat lozenges.

The venues that hosted the World Cup have changed drastically since 1966. The White City, home of so many magical sporting moments, especially from the world of track and field athletics, is no more. Ayresome Park has now been relegated to reserve team football. None of the grounds were all-seater then. Wembley's capacity, for instance, was reduced to 97,000, with seats for 45,000. Everyone was under cover.

At Hillsborough there was a new cantilever stand behind one goal and the capacity was 65,000, all under cover, with seats for 25,000. At Villa Park, one of the stands had been rebuilt, the pitch had been widened and there was room for 54,000 spectators (18,000 seated) with cover for 35,000.

Manchester United, before they knew Old Trafford was to be nominated as one of the venues, set about building a new cantilever stand, which was completed in September 1965, giving the ground a capacity of 64,000, 18,340 seated, with 52,000 of the spectators under cover. Everton cut the capacity at Goodison Park to 65,000, but increased the seating accommodation to 18,000.

Sunderland installed temporary seating to achieve a seating capacity of 14,870 – 9,000 more than usual. There was cover for 25,000, room for 63,000. At the now redundant Ayresome Park, alterations raised the capacity to 46,000, 21,000 under cover, with 8,500 temporary seats added to the 5,300 normal seats.

All was set, then, for the start of what everyone hoped would be a hugely successful tournament.

I have read that the 1966 World Cup was the first to be televised direct, as opposed to delayed or filmed transmission. This is certainly not true. Way back in 1954, World Cup games were televised direct from Switzerland, and I remember the infamous meeting between Brazil and Hungary, which became known as 'The Battle of Berne'. As the aggro was nearing its peak, a violent electrical storm over the Alps cut the line from Switzerland and vision was lost all over Europe for some time.

I immediately switched from a television commentary to a radio one during the break and told the viewers who had lost their picture, 'I'm glad you can't see what's going on. It's disgraceful.' A flood of telephone calls to the BBC and a shoal of letters which awaited me on my return to England proved conclusively that the viewers at home were fuming they had been robbed of a view of the trouble!

Though in the early days television was regarded as football's greatest enemy because it was feared that it would encourage the public to forsake the terraces in favour of a comfortable seat in their own living-room watching matches on the box, television played no small part in bringing the 1966 World Cup to England.

In 1958 Peter Dimmock, Head of Outside Broadcasts at the BBC, heard a whisper that the Football Association was going to bid for the right to stage the finals of the 1966 competition. He decided to take two expert cameramen armed with two electronic cameras to the World Cup in Sweden to supplement the host country's television armoury, to demonstrate to FIFA the BBC's excellence in sports coverage.

FIFA officials were suitably impressed and it is said that from the moment they saw what BBC Television could offer, England had no rivals in the bid to stage the 1966 World Cup.

The two cameramen Peter Dimmock took with him to Sweden were Frank Hudson and Bill Wright, the same Bill Wright who had been loaned to the Swiss television company in 1954 so that he could be their No. 1 cameraman at the first-ever televised World Cup. In fact it was the first time the Eurovision link had been used for anything other than news.

Bill Wright was a great cameraman with whom I worked many times, but he didn't want to remain a cameraman all his life. His great ambition was to break into production. He finally succeeded and he hadn't been in the job very long before he submitted the complete format for a new-style quiz show. The powers-that-be were interested but not ecstatic. They accepted the show for a short run only.

The viewers were more enthusiastic than the BBC. The show got rave reviews and tremendous audience reaction.

Ex-cameraman Bill Wright had a hit on his hands with a programme he had devised and produced himself. The programme was entitled *Mastermind*.

The rest is history. In Bill Wright's capable hands, *Mastermind* quickly became one of the jewels in the BBC's crown and is still running to this day. Sadly Bill Wright is no longer producing it. He died in the prime of his life some years ago. He was a great loss to television.

When the Football Association won the nomination to host the Finals, television faced the mammoth task of beating the biggest challenge it had faced to date – and there were just five years in which to do it.

BBC Television and Independent Television decided to form a consortium to share the task of providing the hardware, such as cameras and the rest of the paraphernalia required for an outside broadcast. The BBC and ITV would work in tandem, with the BBC covering certain grounds, ITV others. Both networks, however, would cover the Final. No one wanted to miss out on that (especially when it turned out to be England against West Germany). The BBC would also be responsible for providing pictures to the world.

We were now in the age of the satellite which had to be used to service the American continent (North and South, where, of course, the interest was at its highest), the Far East, Australia and New Zealand, and to South Africa and those countries on the African continent which were geared to taking the live feed. Other countries, such as those in the Middle East, wanted videotapes of the matches, so within minutes of the final whistle dispatch riders would have to race towards the nearest airport with videotapes for these countries.

Those countries which did not have videotape would be provided with telerecordings, dispatched by air within four to six hours of the final whistle. It was a gigantic task.

Covering all the games stretched both the BBC and ITV to

the limit, and I must admit that when I read through my schedule I wondered whether it was all possible, as the commentators had to be available to conduct interviews and to take part in the special World Cup programmes as well as doing their main job on match days.

My schedule called for me to be at Wembley for the Opening Ceremony followed by the opening game between England and Uruguay on the evening of Monday, 11 July. Then there would be no rest until after the Final on Saturday afternoon, 30 July. It would mean a stint of twelve commentaries in twenty days, plus a lot of travelling.

One thing that worried me when I digested this schedule was that only eighteen months before the World Cup began I had suffered a heart attack. I owe a great debt to West Ham United for the fact that I was around at all in 1966.

It happened at Upton Park in January 1965. West Ham beat Birmingham in a third round FA Cup tie on a cold, damp day, and after the game I was invited into the boardroom – West Ham was one of the really hospitable clubs in those days – and was met by the club doctor. He was a small, Scottish gentleman with a glorious sense of humour who, whenever we met, always turned to the steward in charge of the bar and ordered, 'A large Scotch and water for Kenneth on the National Health.'

The welcome was the same on that dreary January day and as I took my first sip of the whisky the doctor began to enthuse about the game. 'I'm glad you enjoyed it,' was my moaning reply, and the doc gave me a searching look. 'Are you feeling all right?' he asked, and I proceeded to tell him that I felt tired and miserable, that I had indigestion and aches all over.

With that the doc advised me to go home and ring my own doctor. I did go home but I didn't ring my doctor. Instead, whenever the acute 'indigestion' struck, I would swallow a can of beer. That brought relief, but not for long.

The middle of the night brought the classic pain and horrendous perspiration of a heart attack so it was no surprise that the following day I was installed as a patient in St Helier Hospital in Carshalton.

In those days, intensive care was somewhat different than what we know today. It was a case of lying in bed, bell in hand in case I wanted to summon a nurse, and innumerable visits from a variety of medics who all wanted to ram what looked like a six-inch nail into the top of my thumb to produce a drop of blood for testing. It soon became common knowledge that I hated needles, so the nurses (God bless them!) loved to walk into my room armed with a needle, singing the hit song of the day – *Anyone Who Has a Heart*.

Happily, I recovered and after three and a half weeks in hospital I was discharged, having slimmed down from just over 15 stone to 12½ and turned my back on the dreaded narcotic weed they sell as cigarettes.

During the World Cup, as a precaution, I was never without the anti-coagulant tablets and the trinitrates, those tiny, white pills you put under your tongue if and when you feel a pain in the chest.

I had covered three previous World Cups as the commentator for BBC Television: 1954 in Berne, Switzerland, 1958 in Stockholm, Sweden and 1962 in Santiago, Chile. But none of them had anything like the importance of 1966 in London, England.

That isn't a narrow-minded nationalist view because England were the hosts, but simply because this was the biggest television challenge of all time. Yes, my three previous World Cup competitions had been televised, but none of them on the world-wide scale of 1966.

We take so much for granted these days, but thirty years ago the problems were enormous. Luxuries like slow motion were in their infancy. In fact, there was only one machine in the country and it was used at the 1966 World Cup, the first time slow motion had been used in the coverage of a sporting event. The young man who operated the slow motion machine, Jonathan Martin, is now BBC television's head of sport. Zoom lenses didn't come on line until 1965 and the BBC grabbed all the country had for use by the television consortium. There were only thirty-five tape machines in the country by July 1966. The BBC alone needed twenty-six of them for their World Cup coverage.

All this might seem laughable nowadays in an age when television has so much equipment that it would not be surprising if we were to be treated to a picture of a goalkeeper's heart racing just before he faced a penalty kick!

Failure was a word that never entered the thoughts of any of the men and women who worked night and day to ensure the coverage of the World Cup. Nobody bothered about the number of hours they had to work in a day.

Riggers worked in all weathers getting the equipment to the right place and then moving it somewhere else. Thirty years ago the equipment was big, bulky and heavy. Each camera weighed 280 pounds, and needed four men to carry it. Nowadays a rigger can carry two of the modern lightweight cameras at a time!

In the end not a single game in the World Cup 1966 was denied television coverage.

One bitter disappointment for us in television when we knew that the eyes of the world would be on us was that the government would not allow television to transmit the World Cup in colour. Black and white pictures were well and good. In fact they were the only sort of pictures the average television viewer had seen.

The government were told that as long as there was two years' notice, colour transmission was possible, which would obviously greatly enhance the television coverage of the event.

The television set manufacturers, however, lobbied the government, claiming that they were not geared to producing 625 lines sets essential for colour transmission until 1967. That argument won the day, although the more cynical among us would claim that the manufacturers were only trying to buy time to allow them to clear their stocks of the old 405 line sets before introducing the modern 625 lines sets.

Another problem according to the government was that it would have to change the television charter, which at that time only allowed black and white transmission, and there was not enough time to do that.

The government remained adamant so it was left to Mexico, in 1970, to claim the technical achievement which could and would have been Britain's four years earlier but for the lack of foresight by our politicians.

One thing television could not abide in 1966 was the commercialization of sport. No way would they allow any perimeter advertising.

The BBC's charter did not allow it to show advertising; the independent television companies wanted to show only advertisements for which they were being paid.

There was, though, one piece of splendid advertising at Wembley in 1966. On top of the scoreboard to the left as the television cameras looked at the pitch, was the only advertisement ... for the *Radio Times*! It had been there for years!

7

The Path to the Final

Day One

I always feel sorry for the team which have to stage the opening game. They follow the Opening Ceremony, with its speeches, its introductions and its parade of flags of the competing nations carried by youngsters. One begins to think that the football is nothing more than the supporting act. Perhaps it would be a good idea to follow the lead of the Olympic Games and make a vast extravaganza out of the Opening Ceremony, leaving the actual sport until the next day.

However, England and Uruguay did their best to entertain, and it is significant that, while many of the football fans at Wembley thought it a pretty boring encounter, a number of people who watched on television at home for the sake of peace and quiet, thought some of the football was quite beautiful and entertaining.

It was a tight game and chances were hard to engineer. Two fell to Connelly, who was within a whisker of scoring both times, but for the most part England found it difficult to break down the tight Uruguayan defence, which had a splendid sweeper in Troche. Uruguay wanted to play slowly and carefully to stifle England. England wanted to speed things up, and the tactical battle was intriguing, although it produced no goals.

Day Two

It was up to Goodison Park to see the reigning champions, Brazil, against Bulgaria, one of the countries regarded as the whipping boy of the competition. But it didn't turn out that way.

The Bulgarians gave the crowd of 50,000 a shock because they took the game to the champions, and although it never looked as if they would win the match, they made certain that it was no walkover for Brazil. They had a tremendous full back in Shalamanov, who blotted out Jairzinho completely; an elegant midfield player in Yakimov; and a twenty-two-year-old striker called George Asparukhov, who would have given the Brazilian defence an almighty tough evening if he had received a little more support.

But the Brazilians had Pelé, who was in magnificent form and who bent a free-kick from the edge of the penalty area round the wall and way out of the goalkeeper's reach. In the second half, Garrincha scored in similar fashion from another free-kick.

So, were Brazil on the way to retaining their title and making it three World Cups in a row?

Day Three

I was able to get some sort of idea the following evening when Hungary and Portugal played at Old Trafford, and it was good to meet an old friend there in Ferenc Puskás, captain of the eleven stars of the fantastic Hungarian side which thrashed England twice in six months, 6–3 at Wembley in November 1953 and 7–1 in Budapest in May 1954. (I still cannot remember how we got one!) But Puskas was a sad man as he saw his fellow countrymen scorn chance after chance and concede two silly goals to lose the match. The first came after only two minutes from a corner kick. The whole defence was watching Torres, the giant centre forward, but it was José Augusto who rose to head the ball into the net. For the rest of the first half Hungary ran Portugal ragged but wasted many chances, the best one falling to Meszöly, who scooped the ball over an open goal.

Hungary equalized fifteen minutes into the second half when the Portuguese goalkeeper, Carvalho, dropped the ball and Bene prodded it over the line. The lead lasted only a few minutes before the Hungarian goalkeeper fumbled the ball and José Augusto scored his own and his side's second goal. In the very last minute, Torres made it 3–1.

Day Four

Having seen Hungary make so many errors in defence and squander so many opportunities at Old Trafford, one feared for their chances against Brazil at Goodison Park. But the Merseyside supporters in the 52,000 crowd soon made it clear that they were on the side of the Hungarians. Hungary knew that they had to win or go out of the competition and, inspired by the support of the crowd, they raised their game against a Brazil without Pelé, who was unfit, and gave one of their finest displays for some time. In fact, the players were so moved by their reception that Florian Albert, who had a magnificent game at centre forward, said after the match, 'On behalf of the whole team I would like to thank the people of Liverpool for their wonderful support. It was just like playing at home.'

(They probably *wouldn't* have got that sort of support at home because all the sides that have followed the magic team of the Fifties have been viewed with deep suspicion and dissatisfaction by the Hungarian fans. So much so that the game is at a very low ebb in the country today.)

Brazil proved that without Pelé they were like a house without foundations. Garrincha never got into the game and the veteran defenders, Djalma Santos and Bellini, wilted under the relentless Hungarian pressure.

It was a tremendous match which revived memories of the 1954 World Cup in Switzerland. No, not memories of the Battle of Berne, but memories of a superb game in which Hungary beat Uruguay 4–2 after extra-time. People had often wondered who would have won if the best-ever Hungarian side (1954) had met the best-ever Brazilian side, the 1958 World Cup winners. (Later that side would be over-shadowed by the team that was to win in 1970.)

We can never get answers to hypothetical questions, but the meeting in 1966 was something to savour. It had thrills, it had speed and it had beautiful football from both teams. It underlined what everyone had said at the draw in January ... that the two countries eliminated from Group Three would have reached the quarter-finals at least in any other group.

So thrilling was it that Hungary could have been a goal down before Bene put them into the lead after just three minutes. And what a splendid goal it was! He beat the full back and gave himself a shooting chance, but at the last second he cut inside and took on Bellini. This he did success-fully before lashing an unstoppable shot past Gylmar.

Tostão soon equalized and Goodison Park was kept in a state of continual excitement. It could have gone either way, but the knock-out blow came in the sixty-fifth minute. Albert sent Bene away down the right wing, and when Bene crossed the ball about two feet off the ground, Farkas, after a sprint of fully thirty yards, met it on the volley with his right foot and Gylmar never even moved as the shot flashed past him into the net. There was no way back for Brazil after that, and the penalty kick converted later by Meszöly affected only the goal tally, not the result.

Ecstatic post-match discussions about the Hungary *v* Brazil game were stilled when the news came in from the north east: the North Koreans had won their first point. A 1–1 draw with Chile was a splendid performance by the Asians, who had won the hearts of the north-east fans. Chile had gone into the lead with a penalty from Marcos, but Ayresome Park had erupted when Pak Seung Zin equalized.

Football was becoming more of a world-wide game than it ever had been in previous years.

Day Five

Back to Wembley for my fifth game, and it was hard to realize that the World Cup was not yet one week old. This time it was to see England take on Mexico, a match for which Alf Ramsey made two significant changes. Martin Peters came into the midfield in place of Alan Ball, and, though the policy of playing an orthodox winger was continued, Terry Paine was preferred to John Connelly. Connelly was a little unlucky to lose his place after his performance against Uruguay, but Alf Ramsey was a wily old fox and he probably decided to give Connelly and Paine one game each so that he could see which fitted better into his plan.

But Day Five was not a particularly exciting one. In fact, after the champagne of the previous evening, Saturday, 16

The Men of 1966: *back row, l-r* – trainer Les Cocker, George Cohen, Gerry Byrne, Roger Hunt, Ron Flowers, Gordon Banks, Ron Springett, Peter Bonetti, Jimmy Greaves, Bobby Moore, John Connelly, George Eastham and trainer Harold Shepherdson; *front row, l-r* – Jimmy Armfield, Nobby Stiles, Jack Charlton, Geoff Hurst, Terry Paine, Ray Wilson, Martin Peters, Alan Ball and Bobby Charlton; on ground – Norman Hunter (*left*) and Ian Callaghan. (*Hulton Deutsch*)

Jimmy Greaves shoots as France's defenders look on, 20 July 1966. *(Popperfoto)*

In the commentary box with producer Ronnie Noble *(seated, left)*. It doesn't look as if any of us were enjoying this game much!

Two scenes from the quarter finals. *Top:* Alf Ramsey seemingly trying to stop George Cohen from swapping shirts with an Argentinian player after a particularly stormy game. *Bottom:* Portugal's Eusébio is stopped by North Korea's Shin Yung Kyoo and goalkeeper Bi Chan Myung, in an almost unbelievable game that at one point had the great Korean side up by 3–0.

(Popperfoto)

Scenes from England's semi-final against Portugal. *Top:* Eusébio scores Portugal's only goal from the penalty spot. *Below:* Eusébio heads for goal again, watched by Nobby Stiles, but the final score of 2–1 sees England through to the Final, to the great excitement of Stiles and Gordon Banks – and indeed the rest of the nation! *(Popperfoto)*

30 July 1966: England and West Germany, with the match officials, line up for the National Anthems before kick-off. (*Popperfoto*)

Gordon Banks punches the ball away in a tense moment. *(Popperfoto)*

Geoff Hurst heads in England's first goal to level the score. *(Popperfoto)*

The scene after England's disputed third goal: England appeal, Germany protest.
(Popperfoto)

And then it *was* all over. Captain Bobby Moore receives the most coveted trophy in world football from Her Majesty the Queen. (Popperfoto)

Great players and good friends: *Top:* with Gordon Banks, a true hero of 1966. *Below, left:* with West Germany's goal-scoring centre back Wolfgang Weber at the 25th anniversary of the 1966 World Cup Final; *right:* with everybody's World Cup hero, Bobby Moore, at the House of Commons launch of *It's Twelve Inches High*, a book produced in aid of charity.

July produced nothing more palatable than mild beer. There were four games, 360 minutes of football and only six goals, three of which were scored by Portugal against Bulgaria, who were now on their way out of the reckoning.

Another two goals were scored by England, who thus broke their duck. It wasn't an exhilarating performance, but as Alf Ramsey said afterwards, 'It is never easy to play when the opposition crowds the penalty area with eight defenders.'

Prospective World Cup winners have to do just that, though, hard as it may be, and against Mexico England were happy to give thanks to Bobby Charlton for putting them into the lead with a goal no one will ever forget. After thirty-seven frustrating minutes, Charlton got the ball in his own half and set off towards the Mexican goal. The Mexicans fell back to crowd their penalty area, but Charlton resisted the temptation to carry the ball into that built-up zone. From fully thirty yards he released a right-foot shot which flew into the net with the speed and accuracy of an Exocet missile.

It was a goal of the highest quality, typical of Bobby Charlton at his most exciting best, and I was delighted to realize, when I saw the television replay, that I anticipated Bobby's shot in my commentary a split second before he released it.

Charlton was involved in the second goal a quarter of an hour before the end. It was his pass which sent Greaves away, and when Calderon beat down his shot, Roger Hunt was there to tap it into the net.

Villa Park staged a disappointing, bad-tempered game between the two favourites, Argentina and West Germany. It was just a dour, defensive battle, and battle is the operative word because neutral observers thought that Jorge Albrecht, of Argentina, should not have been the only player sent off by the Yugoslav referee.

In the other games, Portugal strolled to a 3–0 victory over Bulgaria, which put them out of the competition, and a single goal was enough to give Russia victory over Italy in a defence-dominated game at Roker Park. This meant that Russia were safely through to the next stage and that Italy would join them if they beat North Korea.

Day Six

The game everyone wanted to see on this day was the one at Goodison Park – Brazil *v* Portugal. Sadly, I wasn't one of the 58,479 people lucky enough to be there, but you can't win them all!

I was at a very wet Wembley with 35,000 others – a surprisingly large crowd – to see Mexico and Uruguay meander through a goalless draw which was, nevertheless, enough to get Uruguay through to the quarter-finals, albeit with the unimpressive record of two goalless draws and a 2–1 victory in three games.

Meanwhile, at Goodison Park an era ended, Brazil were beaten 3–1 by Portugal and, barring a sensationally big win by Bulgaria over Hungary, this meant that the reigning champions were out. As Brazil left the pitch, the crowd rose to them and the Portuguese players stood and applauded them to the dressing-room.

Without doubt, Portugal were worthy winners. Brazil had failed to produce a settled side after their three-month training stint, and while the old hands like Bellini, Djalma Santos and Garrincha could no longer stand the pace, some of the replacements were too inexperienced. But Brazil, a nation which had given football so much freshness and excitement over the last eight years, went out with dignity.

Brazil went into the match knowing that if Hungary beat Bulgaria (which we all expected) a three-goal win over Portugal was necessary to keep the champions in the competition. Forced to field an inexperienced side, they nevertheless decided to play in their usual free, attacking, exciting Brazilian way. They had always scorned the move towards dull, negative defensive tactics, and even this time, when they knew in their heart of hearts that they were not good enough to make the grade, they refused to fall back on destroying tactics so popular in many other places.

Brazil's defence was pulled apart by four Portuguese forwards, magnificently led by Eusébio, undoubtedly the Man of the Match. Brazil put their hopes in some Pelé magic to turn the game their way, but Pelé failed, or to put it more correctly, Pelé was never allowed to succeed.

He had been battered enough in the game against Bulgaria and was unable to play against Hungary because of an injured knee. Against Portugal he was shadowed by three men and twice was cruelly chopped down by dreadful tackles. The first one was punished by nothing more than a free kick. The second earned the culprit a talking-to from the referee, but that didn't matter. Pelé was taken off and returned with his heavily bandaged knee reducing him to a limping passenger. (No substitutions were allowed in those days.)

Portugal had proved themselves a side that could and well might go through to win the trophy. And Brazil were out of the tournament.

If it was sad to see Brazil go out of the competition, it was sensational to see Italy follow them. But follow them they did after an amazing 1–0 defeat by North Korea at Ayresome Park, a shock result to rival England's defeat at the hands of the United States in Belo Horizonte, Brazil, in 1950.

Day Seven

And so it was on to the seventh day of the tournament, judgement day. Mind you, by this time, most of the questions had been answered. One that hadn't was, 'Where will England finish?' So far the host nation had gained three points from two games. A win or a draw against France would put them in first place above Uruguay, but a defeat would land them in second place and a quarter-final against West Germany!

Ninety-two and a half thousand people packed Wembley to cheer England on to victory, and they saw winger No. 3 take his place in the side. Ian Callaghan took over from Terry Paine. Certainly nobody could now claim that Alf Ramsey didn't play wingers!

France had no realistic chance of qualifying. They would have to beat England by a rugby score, and as England hadn't conceded a goal and looked to have the strongest defence of the sixteen starters, there was little chance of that happening.

Whatever faint hope might have existed in optimistic French hearts disappeared early on. Robert Herbin, the midfield player, injured his knee and spent the rest of the evening hobbling around as a passenger. Yet the French always strove to play good football and made a worthy contribution to the best game we had seen in Group One.

It was a hard enough struggle for the French in the first half with only ten fit men, and they must have cringed five minutes before half-time when Jack Charlton headed against an upright and Hunt had the easiest of tasks to score from the rebound.

Even though one down, the French continued to make a game of it and were still in with a shout until the seventy-fifth minute when a particularly bad tackle by Stiles left Simon in agony.

The incredible thing was that the referee waved play on and, with Simon still on the ground, Callaghan centred and Hunt headed the goal that put the result beyond doubt. Simon returned to the field after treatment, his knee heavily bandaged, but he played no useful part in the rest of the game.

England deserved to win the match, but the French injuries took some of the gilt off the gingerbread. No one could understand why the referee had taken no action over the foul on Simon, for foul it certainly was. At the very least the French should have had a free kick and they would still have been in the game, just one down with fifteen minutes remaining. And without any doubt, Stiles deserved a caution for his tackle.

Only later did we discover that Stiles *was* cautioned by the referee. Some accounts of the match say that he wasn't but that he was reported to the Disciplinary Committee by the Match Commissar. That is not correct. The announcement from the Disciplinary Committee states:

The FIFA Disciplinary Committee under the Chairmanship of Mr M. S. L. Maduro considered reports which had been received from matches since their last meeting.

In Match 21, France *v* England, England No. 4 Stiles was cautioned by the referee. The Committee decided to send a letter to the Football Association intimating that if the player is reported to the Committee again, either by a referee or by the Official Commissar for a match serious action will be taken.

It was obvious from that statement that another transgression by Stiles would mean the end of his World Cup.

Alf Ramsey asked Stiles a couple of days before the quarter-final whether he had meant to foul Simon. Stiles' reply was honest and to the point: 'No, I didn't mean it, but he turned too quickly for me and it ended up a horrendous tackle. But I didn't mean it. It was just bad timing.' That was enough for Ramsey and there was never any danger of Nobby being dropped from the side.

(The two players met a few years after the World Cup and Simon assured Stiles that the injury wasn't as bad as it was at first feared and that he was playing again inside a month. The players parted friends.)

France were not the only team to suffer casualties in the match. Greaves received a severe cut on the shin, and that was to become the most discussed injury in World Cup football. Well, in England it certainly was – and still is.

At Villa Park, Spain had to win the game to stay in the competition (at the expense of West Germany) and they decided to go for broke and leave out such stars as Del Sol, Gento, Peiro and Suarez. The changes were so successful that Spain produced their best performance yet, but it was all too little, too late. At least they scored against the Germans, something no other side had been able to do, and for about ten minutes after Fuste's goal, Spain were in the lead and had heady ideas about qualification. These were dashed by Emmerich's equalizer and Seeler's winner. West Germany beat Spain 2–1, and that was enough to clinch the top spot in the group.

At Old Trafford it looked for a short time as if a miracle would happen and Bulgaria would beat Hungary and give Brazil a reprieve. But it wasn't to be.

Bulgaria scored first through their excellent centre forward, Asparukhov, but just before half-time, Hungary equalized with one of those goals everyone laughs about, except the team conceding it. Davidov, the Bulgarian goalkeeper, cleared the ball but it hit one of his colleagues and rebounded into the net!

There was still time for Meszöly to put Hungary 2–1 up at the interval and in the second half Bene clinched it.

Up in the north east, Russia joined Portugal as a one hundred per cent team although they played more or less their second squad against Chile.

The Quarter-Finals

The four quarter-finals were all played on the same day, Saturday, 23 July. West Germany were up against Uruguay at Hillsborough, Portugal faced the remarkable North Koreans at Goodison Park, Roker Park staged Russia against Hungary, while at Wembley there was England against Argentina, a match which would become memorable (for all the wrong reasons).

The games at Wembley and Goodison Park overshadowed the other two, and the one at Goodison Park nearly produced the most unbelievable result of all time. I was at Wembley and suddenly heard over the earphones, 'There's a scoreline that North Korea are leading Portugal 3–0 but don't mention it because someone has probably got it the wrong way round.' That news raised a smile or two in our cramped commentary position and soon after Wembley was drenched by a shower of laughter. The scoreboard gave us the news: 'Portugal 0–North Korea 3.' Not a soul among the 88,000 spectators believed it, but confirmation soon came through that 0–3 was, indeed, the correct score.

Everyone had laughed when North Korea qualified for the final stage of the World Cup. Some people even said they wouldn't turn up. But Sir Stanley Rous was adamant. 'North

Korea will turn up,' he promised, 'and they will surprise a lot of people.'

Surprise a lot of people they certainly did, but they delighted even more with their happy-go-lucky approach to the game. They lost their first match to Russia, but, undaunted, took on Chile and held them to a draw. They then dropped a bombshell by beating Italy, sending them home to be met by a hail of tomatoes thrown at the humiliated players by the irate fans. For the North Koreans it was more than they could have hoped for in their wildest dreams.

But against Portugal? Surely they hadn't got a hope in front of 42,248 fans at Goodison Park. Hadn't they? They came out and played quick, simple football which tore so many holes in the Portuguese defence that in twenty-five minutes they were 3–0 up. With the spectators chanting, 'We want four' the North Koreans ran around, smiles creasing their faces.

Then something akin to an earthquake hit them. That something was Eusébio. He started to show the sort of player he really was, and that was fatal for Korea. He scored a goal, and then, when Torres was brought down, he scored a second from the penalty spot. So it was 3–2 to the North Koreans at half-time.

But the Korean party was over. Within fifteen minutes of the second half starting, Eusébio had not only equalized but had put Portugal ahead. Later on he floated across the centre from which José Augusto headed in the fifth.

So it was Portugal who progressed to the semi-final stage. But the North Koreans left behind them a host of happy memories before they went home to re-enter their state of not-so-splendid isolation. What a pity we didn't see more of them in the following years.

Wembley should have been a stadium of skill on this Saturday afternoon, 23 July, just seven days from the Final. Instead it was the venue of violence. England and Argentina had always been regarded as two teams who could have been right there at the end. But even before the kick-off there were factors which put a blight on the game.

After the severe warning given to England about Stiles' tackle on Simon and the subsequent caution, England were apprehensive. Argentina were more than apprehensive at the appointment of a West German referee, Rudolf Kreitlein, in view of the fact that the only sending-off so far in the competition had been an Argentine, Jorge Albrecht, in the match against West Germany.

In the first minute an English player was chopped down by an Argentine. This was a great chance for Mr Kreitlein to stamp his authority on the game but he chickened out. All he did was award a free kick. It was a fatal error of judgement, and within minutes the referee had lost control of the game completely. He closed his eyes to some of the crudest tackles you could imagine. Violence was being allowed.

However, Ferreiro, Solari and Albrecht went into the book for nothing more heinous than childishly kicking the ball away after the award of a free kick, and Rattin was booked for a minor foul on Bobby Charlton.

After Albrecht was booked, Rattin, the Argentine captain, appeared to say something to the referee. He told me later that all he did was ask for an interpreter so that he could ask a question. Mayhem broke out as Mr Kreitlein ordered Rattin off the field. The Argentine refused to go, and his team-mates made it plain that it was a case of 'if Rattin goes, we all go.'

Ken Aston, FIFA's referees' liaison officer intervened. So, too, did Harry Cavan, of Northern Ireland and a member of FIFA, and a couple of Argentine officials. Eventually Rattin decided that there was no point in squabbling any longer and he left the field, sent off obviously for 'violence of the tongue.'

Play, if you can call it that, resumed after the ten-minute hold-up, and from then onwards it was a case of 'if it moves, kick it.' All the skill the Argentines possessed was scattered to the winds, and the calmest and fairest player on the field was Nobby Stiles.

We were spared extra-time when, thirteen minutes from the end, Peters crossed a perfect centre and his clubmate Hurst, making his World Cup début, headed in the only goal of a best forgotten match.

After the game I spoke to Alf Ramsey in the Interview Room and Alf was so disgusted with the behaviour of the Argentine players, that he called them animals. Our conversation was relayed to the Press Room and, although Alf later apologized, the Argentines never forgot or forgave what he said.

Strangely enough, Rattin, who was loudly booed when he walked to the dressing-room, was almost fêted when he was spotted in the streets of London the following day! People wanted to shake his hand and buy him a drink which must have puzzled him enormously given the hostile reaction of the fans at Wembley and the universally unfavourable newspaper reports.

(But I remember something similar happening with the roles reversed in 1968 when Manchester United played Estudiantes de la Plata in the first leg of the European–South American Cup in the Boca Juniors Stadium in Buenos Aires. Nobby Stiles was sent off, and he was loudly booed and also pelted with anything that came to the spectators' hands as he walked round the pitch to the dressing-rooms. The next morning he went shopping in the city and the Argentines mobbed him. I wish I understood psychology!)

We had never heard Antonio Rattin's side of the story until this year when the video company C-21-C interviewed him for a video they were making entitled 'We Wuz Robbed.' They have given me permission to reproduce the interview.

Question: Why did you not leave the field when the referee told you to?
Answer: I didn't leave the field, first of all because I couldn't understand the language. I was asking for an interpreter to clarify some things with the referee.

He was making some decisions that from my point of view as captain of the team were not correct. We also have to bear in mind that, at that time, there were no red cards or yellow cards. The referees only made a gesture with their hands. I asked for an interpreter, which is an international word, but he did not want to understand me. He did not want to listen to what I had to say to him, and then he made the decision of sending me off.
Question: Why were you constantly arguing with the referee during the match?
Answer: I repeat there was no dialogue with the referee, who was German. I spoke Spanish. We couldn't understand each other. But, obviously we are talking about 1966. At that time it was common practice that the home team was always given some advantage or help to get to the Final, and there was no satellite television then. I believe England had a good team, and they didn't need any help at all, but the referee was awarding things that were not right at all. That made me ask for an interpreter so that we could talk things over and then go on normally with the match. But the referee did not understand me, or he did not want to understand or … I don't know, I don't know what might have been the interests

behind all this. And he sent me off, so in the end I had to leave the field!

Question: What interests made the referee favour England?

Answer: Well, every time they ask me about the World Cup, I always feel it necessary to make a difference between World Cups with satellite television and World Cups without satellite television. Sometimes people do not understand why I say this, but it is very easy. FIFA, before satellite television was invented, always favoured the teams which organized the matches, so that they won the Cup or at least got to the Final. And you can prove this. It happened with Sweden, who were the runners-up in 1958, although they have always been really bad in football. The same thing happened in Chile in 1962. From 1970, when satellite arrived in Mexico, everything changed. FIFA started to know the financial benefits they could make from the World Cup. Already they know how many millions of dollars they are going to get from the television of the next World Cup in France. Also, when the referees were assigned, the Argentinian delegates were told the event would take place at 19.00 hours, but when the Argentinian and Uruguayan delegates arrived at the conference they were told the choice had already been made at 18.00 hours.

The referees were chosen without any Argentinian or Uruguayan officials present. A German referee was chosen for the match England *v* Argentina and he sent me off. An English referee was chosen for the Uruguay v West Germany game and he sent off two Uruguayans and made a penalty decision which favoured the Germans.

Question: Do you think that Argentinian footballers have a bad name?

Answer: No, not at all. I don't think so. Argentinian football is spread around the world. We export more than a hundred players a year to Europe and America. The Argentinian players adapt themselves to any climate and any conditions and that is very important. And in some football teams around the world there are always some important Argentinian players. I do not think that Argentinians are natural fighters, or strong individuals, although they have their temperament. They want to win as it is natural with everyone who takes part in a competition.

I always wanted to win, but to win within the law, not to win in an unappropriate manner, not to win if the team we are playing against is superior to us. That's why I think Argentinian football is well considered all around the world. There are Argentinian players in Japan, in Germany, in Holland, in Spain, in Italy and in America.

That, then, is the view of Antonio Rattin, not in the heat of the moment but thirty years after the violent incidents at Wembley. He has been misinformed about, or has misunderstood, the situation regarding the choice of referees. I am assured the refereeing appointments are decided in private and no team delegates are present at the time.

Rattin has a point about interpreters. We all know the frustrations of meeting someone who cannot speak or understand our language. There is no hope of contact, and it is even worse in the heady atmosphere of an important football match. No one, of course, is entitled to argue with the referee or to question his decisions, but it is conceivable that the captain of a side may want some clarification of an incident or a decision. Would it be beyond the capabilities of FIFA to have an interpreter on hand at every important match? All it needs is someone who can speak the languages of the two teams and the referee.

Would we not have been spared a lot of ill-will if a Spanish- and German-speaking individual had walked on to the pitch, found out what was worrying Mr Rattin and sorted out the problem within seconds?

Rattin's worry about satellite and non-satellite matches might well be worthy of consideration. I don't think he meant satellite television as such, but rather the use of satellites for transmission of television pictures on a world-wide basis to terrestrial television networks.

It is interesting to look back at the results of World Cups to date:

1930: host nation Uruguay. Final: Uruguay 4–Argentina 2
1934: host nation Italy. Final: Italy 2–Czechoslovakia 1
1938: host nation France. Final Italy 4–Hungary 2
1950: host nation Brazil. Final Uruguay 1st and Brazil 2nd
   (Uruguay beat Brazil 2–1 in the last game of the four-team
   final pool.)
1954: host nation Switzerland. Final West Germany 3–
   Hungary 2
1958: host nation Sweden. Final Brazil 5–Sweden 2
1962: host nation Chile. Final Brazil 3–Czechoslovakia 1
1966: host nation England. Final England 4–West Germany 2

All the above were non-satellite World Cups.

1970: host nation Mexico. Final Brazil 4–Italy 1
1974: host nation West Germany. Final West Germany 2–
   Holland 1
1978: host nation Argentina. Final Argentina 3–Holland 1
1982: host nation Spain. Final Italy 3–West Germany 1
1986: host nation Mexico. Final Argentina 3–West Germany 2

1990: host nation Italy. Final West Germany 1–Argentina 0
1994: host nation USA. Final Brazil 0–Italy 0 (Brazil won on
 penalties)

So what does that show us? There have been six non-satellite
tournaments and one part-satellite (1966). Three were
won by the host nation (Uruguay, Italy and England), twice
the host nation were runners-up (Brazil and Sweden) and
once the host nation was beaten in the semi-final. Only in
1954 did the host nation – Switzerland – fail to reach the
semi-final.

There have been seven satellite tournaments and the host
nation has won only twice (West Germany and Argentina),
no host nation was runner-up, but one host nation (Italy in
1990) reached the semi-final and finished third.

Those statistics seem to suggest Rattin has a point.

Away from Wembley and Rattin, at Roker Park, Hungary
bade farewell to the 1966 World Cup when two errors by
their goalkeeper, Gelei, cost them the match against Russia. It
was the old Hungarian story. In 1954, a goalkeeping error set
them on the way to defeat in the Final; in 1958, they were
eliminated through goalkeeping errors; in 1962, it was the
same story. Now 1966.

The errors against Portugal, when they lost 3–1 in the first-
round pool, had been bad enough, but the errors against
Russia were worse and cost Hungary, the more attractive
side, a semi-final spot. After only five minutes Gelei dropped
the ball and allowed Chislenko to put Russia ahead, and just
after half-time Gelei completely missed a centre to present
Russia with their second goal. Although Bene did score a
goal for Hungary, there was no road back for them.

And so the semi-final line-up was England *v* Portugal at Wembley and West Germany *v* Russia at Goodison Park.

The Semi-Finals

On Merseyside there were bitter recriminations. They had always believed that England, if they reached that stage, would play their semi-final at Goodison Park. FIFA replied that they couldn't understand how that idea had arisen because they had always insisted that the semi-final venues would not be chosen until the semi-finalists were known.

The reason for this decision was that FIFA had blundered in Chile four years previously in announcing the semi-final venues before knowing the teams concerned. As it happened, Vina del Mara ended up staging the Czechoslovakia *v* Yugoslavia game before a mere 20,000 people, an embarrassing howler for the organizers.

But in 1962 Vina del Mar was the No. 2 venue and was obviously in line for one of the semi-finals. The other semi-final was just as obviously to be in the National Stadium in Santiago, where the capacity was 80,000. Apart from Czechoslovakia and Yugoslavia, the other two semi-finalists were Chile and Brazil. Does anyone seriously suggest that the Chile *v* Brazil game should have been played at the No. 2 venue? To do that would have been more than an embarrassing howler.

Goodison Park, then, lost the chance of playing host to England, and FIFA's feeble explanation only inflamed the anger felt in Lancashire. How much better it would have been if FIFA had admitted that the England *v* Portugal semi-final was given to Wembley because it was more likely to attract a full house than West Germany *v* Russia.

The Merseysiders showed their resentment by staging an unofficial boycott of the Goodison Park semi-final on Monday evening, 25 July, for which only 38,273 turned up, Goodison's lowest attendance of the World Cup.

Those who stayed away must have known a thing or two because it was a disappointing game between two teams which played without passion and without flair. The twenty-two players were like well-drilled automatons, and the tough tackling and blatant obstructions called for a sterner referee than Italy's Lo Bello.

The tackling took its toll and, as early as the fifth minute, Sabo made a clumsy apology of a tackle on Beckenbauer and came off the worst, being reduced to a hobbling passenger for the rest of the ninety minutes. That was a severe, self-inflicted blow to Russia's hopes, and they received another just on half-time when Mr Lo Bello decided it was time to show who was the boss and sent Chislenko off the field. That meant that Russia were down to only nine fit men.

Inevitably they lost, 2–1, with Haller and Beckenbauer scoring for the Germans and Porkujan getting a consolation goal two minutes from the end. It would have been more than 2–1 but for a splendid goalkeeping display by Lev Yashin.

Nobody doubted that West Germany deserved to have made the Final at Wembley but people began to wonder why, of the five players sent off in the competition so far, four of them had been sent off while playing against West Germany – Albrecht (Argentina), Troche (Uruguay), Silva (Uruguay) and Chislenko (Russia). The fifth player to be sent off was Rattin, of Argentina, against England. The referee in that match came from West Germany!

So to the evening of Tuesday, 26 June and the clash between England and Portugal. This was, without doubt

THE game of the competition. This was class, this was excitement and this was football, the beautiful game. These were the twenty-two players who delighted the 90,000 spectators:

ENGLAND: Banks; Cohen, Jack Charlton, Moore, Wilson; Stiles, Bobby Charlton, Peters; Ball, Hunt, Hurst. PORTUGAL: Pereira; Festa, Baptista, José Carlos, Hilário; Graça, Coluna, José Augusto; Eusébio, Torres, Simões.

The names of those twenty-two players should be carved in stone because they produced *the* match of the World Cup, a veritable feast of football best described by the Portuguese coach, Otto Glória, who, when asked after the match who would win the Final, answered, 'Surely this was the Final tonight.'

Everybody played their part in a great occasion, a memorable evening. The Wembley fans were, of course, mainly behind England, but they were highly appreciative of Portugal.

Alf Ramsey had always said that when England met a side willing to come out and play football they would hit their real form. Portugal did come out and play football – brilliant football. England responded in kind, and I remember saying at the time that Bobby Charlton proved himself the nearest thing to Alfredo di Stefano that I had ever seen. He scored both the England goals and Emilio Osterreicher, the former Real Madrid manager who, at that time was managing Español of Barcelona, said, 'I tried to take Bobby Charlton to Real Madrid but failed. He can join me at Español any time he likes.'

Sheer opportunism brought Charlton his first goal after Pereira had partially saved a shot from Hunt, but in the second half Portugal were getting on top ... until Charlton struck again twelve minutes from the end. Cohen sent Hurst away down the right and he pulled the ball back for Charlton to hammer it into the net.

The sportsmanship shown throughout the game was underlined when the Portuguese players applauded Charlton all the way back to the centre circle for the re-start. That didn't mean Portugal were conceding defeat. Far from it. They threw everything into attack and within three minutes won a penalty kick. Nobody saved penalties taken by Eusébio. Banks was no exception.

Encouraged by their goal, Portugal were attacking right to the final whistle, but England hung on to win 2–1, and they couldn't have done it against worthier opponents.

The stage was set for a dream Final … England *v* West Germany.

8

The Glorious 30th July

Saturday, 30 July 1966 is a date lodged in my memory for ever. When I arrived at the stadium between nine o'clock and half-past all was peaceful. Yes, the usual vendors were setting up their stalls; the odd ticket tout had arrived; a few foreign visitors were getting out at Wembley Park station – but it was really the calm before the storm.

You might wonder why I arrived so early for a three-o'clock kick-off. All I can say is that I hate rushing. If I am travelling by car I always leave myself plenty of time, to cope with roadworks, traffic jams or any other unforeseen holdup. If I am travelling by rail, the train is still being cleaned when I arrive at the station, and if I am going by air I try to check in a good hour before the recommended time. As a famous golfer once said: just take time off to smell the flowers.

Anyway time never dragged. There was so much to do, so much to be talked about, so much to check.

The rest of the BBC Television team had arrived even earlier than I did. Alec Weeks was the producer. When he joined the Corporation as a messenger boy, I don't suppose he ever dreamed for one fleeting second that he would one day be the man in charge of the team who would present to the world the biggest sporting spectacle ever seen on television.

It would be impossible to mention every member of our team that day. I wish I could because television is as much a team game as is football itself. To produce a successful programme there cannot be any weak links.

I remember one FA Cup Final in the pre-'Sponsored by Littlewoods Pools' days when Alan Chivers, who directed the match on which I did my very first commentary, was in charge. Just as the two teams were walking up the tunnel on their way to the pitch, every monitor on the television gantry went dead. We were transmitting not only to the United Kingdom but to the whole Eurovision network and the monitors could not have picked a more inopportune moment to desert us. As the teams walk on to the pitch, television always shows close-ups of various players, but with no monitor how would the commentators know which players?

Once the players are in position for the presentations there are more problems. The presentation party has to be identified. So has each player and official as the guest of honour walks down the two lines. A commentator with no monitor is helpless.

As Alan Chivers said over the talkback system, which is heard by everyone, 'All monitors have gone down,' I froze. This is where teamwork came into action. Those who could do something to rectify the situation got to work. I was reassured by Alan's next words: 'Right, we're working on it, Kenneth. In the meantime we're going to a close-up of so-and-so.' From then onwards he told me which player he had in close-up and talked me through the whole presentation ceremony. Just before the kick-off, the monitors sprang into life again.

Not a single soul among the twenty million audience or the hierarchy at Television Centre had a whiff of suspicion that anything had been wrong.

Nevertheless, we all prayed that nothing similar would happen on 30 July 1966, and to the best of my knowledge nothing did. But then, if it didn't affect my part in the operation, I probably wouldn't have known, even though the commentator can hear the producer's voice giving instructions throughout, so that if, for instance, a camera goes on the blink, the commentator will know immediately.

It takes a bit of practice to be able to deliver a commentary with lots of two-, three- or even four-way conversations belting into your ear through the headphones, but once you've mastered the art you've got yourself a useful social asset. You will be able to carry on a conversation in a crowded room, in a pub, in a bar or anywhere else, and at the same time listen to another. It is surprising what you can learn ...

On that exciting July morning, Alec Weeks was rehearsing the technical staff. Nothing, absolutely nothing could be left to chance. As he faced a battery of monitors which showed him what pictures each camera could provide, he had by his side Sheila Davies, his assistant. With them was Ted Bragg, the chief engineer, who could never make his mind up whether he enjoyed the World Cup Final or the Open Golf Championship the best. But, Cup Final or Open Championship, he was a master of his job, which was as difficult as it was complicated.

The team the BBC assembled for the big day at Wembley was one worthy of the occasion. We played our strongest side, as did England and West Germany. The seven cameramen covering the game were: Maurice Abel, Barry Chaston, Harry Coventry, Selwyn Cox, Ken Moir, Keith Williams and

Derek Wright. Two men with whom I worked closely on the day were Peter Massey and Roy Norton, the stage managers, who were the visual link between the scanner and the television gantry on which the commentators worked.

Also on the television gantry were Cameras 1 and 2. Camera 3 was at Exit 37, Camera 4 was in 'the pit' (actually the pit was a hole dug at the side of the pitch), Camera 5 was on the scoreboard in front of the *Radio Times* advertisement. The two remaining cameras, numbers 6 and 7, were positioned low down behind each goal.

The television gantry was perhaps the most crowded part of Wembley Stadium. In fact, there is no perhaps about it. It WAS the most crowded part. The gantry was just underneath the roof of the stand opposite the Royal Box stand and was reached by way of a bumpy lift in which I never had one hundred per cent confidence. Within seconds of it leaving the ground there was an almighty clanging noise which terrified newcomers and to which I never became fully accustomed.

Both the BBC and ITV had relatively comfortable studios for the use of their various analysts. These were managers and players past and present whom the two networks, finding themselves in a head-to-head battle for the audience, had signed up to watch the matches and then comment on the games, the players and the referees. The rest of the gantry was divided into tiny commentary boxes into which commentators from all over the world were shoehorned so tightly that the monitors had to be placed to one side. Walley Barnes, with whom I had worked so often and got on well, was my summarizer. He had to squeeze in behind me and, if my memory serves me right, had to stand throughout the match if he wanted to see anything at all! So please don't run away with the idea that television commentators worked in the lap of luxury.

Before we all got into that rickety lift which took us to our positions, where, to put it as delicately as possible, there were 'no facilities', we had lunch and a briefing session.

The briefing session was mainly for our colleagues from abroad, and I must admit that us commentators had become something of a club, meeting often for many fine matches at many interesting venues. They all seemed to possess a remarkable command of the English language, which left us Brits ashamed at our lack of linguistic proficiency. I was particularly impressed by the fluent English of Tomas Vitray, the Hungarian commentator, who has always been a great friend of mine.

During the celebrations in Budapest – to which I was very proud to be invited – of the fortieth anniversary of Hungary's 6–3 victory over England at Wembley in 1953, Tomas Vitray interviewed the surviving players from both teams equally fluently in Hungarian and English.

People often ask me what Wembley was like on World Cup Final day. I can only answer that it was just like a carnival. Ninety-three thousand people were at Wembley for the 1966 World Cup Final, with gate receipts of a then record of £200,000.

As I look back thirty years it is amazing to realize the immense financial changes that have taken place in the game. For Euro 96 tickets, it is anticipated that total sales will exceed £100 million.

But then Euro 96 tickets cost from £15 to £130, whereas a friend of mine in 1966 had a seat near the Royal Box at every London game (nine at Wembley, including the semi-final between England and Portugal and the Final itself, and one at the White City) at a cost of just £15. A programme, which included a picture and details of every player in every one of the sixteen squads, cost two shillings and sixpence, or 12½ pence.

In the programme you could find out that Tudor World Cup crisps cost a shilling a packet (that is five pence), Player's No. 6 cigarettes were three shillings and sixpence (17½ pence) for twenty and there was a new after-shave called Mennen for four shillings and sixpence (22½p).

The players received a match fee of £60, and as a reward for the final victory, each of the twenty-two squad members was given a bonus of £1,000. This bonus and the match fee was subject to the basic rate of tax of 41.5 per cent.

It is very easy to become confused when comparing 1966 prices to those of today, but a friend of mine in the City advised me that, as a general rule, £1 in 1966 would be worth around £10 or £12 today. So my fee of £60 for commentating on the 1966 Final (no overtime for extra-time!) would be worth £600 today. The average weekly wage then was £20.5s (£20.25p), equivalent to £202.5p today – though, in fact, the average weekly wage today is £336.30. The lowest price for a standing position at a top league game was five shillings (25p) which is equivalent to £2.50p today; a loaf of bread would set you back 10p, or £1 today; a pint of bitter was 9p so should be 90p today; a bottle of Scotch whisky was £2.42p so it should be £24.20 today.

A car so evocative of the 1960s, the Mini, would have set you back £479 in 1966.

If it was a trip to the theatre you wanted, in 1966 you could follow the crowds to Anna Neagle and Joe Brown in *Charlie Girl* or head off to the Manchester Hippodrome for *The Sound of Music*.

If the Manchester hills were alive with the sound of music, radios all over the country were alive with the sound of Tom

Jones dreaming of *The Green, Green Grass of Home*, Jim Reeves was hearing those *Distant Drums* and Frank Sinatra's *Strangers in the Night* was slightly ahead of daughter Nancy Sinatra's boots, which were made for walking. There were some other super songs around: *Yellow Submarine* (didn't Chelsea adopt that as their theme song?), *Paperback Writer* and that glorious Walker Brothers' hit, *The Sun Ain't Gonna Shine Anymore*.

Not a bad year for looking and listening.

At Wembley for the Final there were no barriers to cage in the spectators, and there was no segregation. How could there be? In World Cups – and European Championships – tickets are sold on a series basis and no one can be sure who will play in the Final.

Although there will always be troublemakers, none were in evidence at Wembley. Everybody was friendly, bent on having a great afternoon's enjoyment. The Germans turned up with their banners advertising which area of Germany they originated from and they were armed with nothing more lethal than the inevitable hunting horns, which made a deafening noise. But the English, with their chants of 'England! England!' won the decibel battle. It was all good-natured with the only disappointing sight, perhaps, that of some English fans failing to realize that the Union Flag is not the English flag. (It would have been churlish to point out to the Eurovision commentators that they were using the wrong flag when so many English people made the same mistake!) Sooner or later, I hope it will dawn on all English fans that the Union Flag is the flag of the United Kingdom and that the flag of England is the St George's Cross.

I must admit I was a little apprehensive when I read Vincent Mulchrone's column in the *Daily Mail*, on the morning of the match. He wrote: 'If Germany beat us at Wembley this afternoon at our national sport, we can always point out to them that we have recently beaten them twice at theirs.' It was hardly what we wanted to read in one of our leading newspapers on the morning of a football match, especially one as important as the Final of the World Cup.

Perhaps there was a little animosity towards the Germans, but it was shown mainly by those people from countries which had been occupied during the war. In fact, some of the European commentators draped a Union Flag from the front of my position and added, 'You mustn't lose this one.'

I remember walking from the dressing-room area, up the tunnel and round the track something like an hour before I was due to go on air. At last we had reached the day of the Final. It had not been an uneventful journey. There had been hiccups along the way. First, television had to shrug off the huge disappointment of not being allowed by the government to cover the competition in colour, though the BBC allowed itself one act of defiance. It was determined to show the world that colour transmission was possible in 1966, so it installed on the television gantry at Wembley a colour camera and a colour video recorder under the control of an engineer, Norman Taylor. It worked a treat!

The next problem had involved the planned display by the Massed Bands of the Brigade of Guards (and how much more impressive that would have been if it could have been seen in full colour).

Service bandsmen, like all professional musicians, are members of the Musicians' Union. As such they are entitled to be paid a fee for all engagements which are not State Occasions. World Cup matches at Wembley were not regarded as State Occasions and a couple of weeks or so before the Opening Ceremony the Musicians' Union pointed out to television officials that each bandsman would be entitled to a fee of £10 an appearance, plus another £10 if the transmission went to any overseas countries.

That was a body blow to television because the Massed Bands of the Brigade of Guards were to be an important part of the entertainment at Wembley. And, as the Massed Bands were comprised of 200 men, the Union's claim would have meant an unexpected additional expenditure of £4,000 for the Final alone. That sort of money did not exist in anyone's budget. (Incidentally, I am told that £4,000 in 1966 is equivalent to £70,000 in today's money.)

(And the problem did not just affect Wembley. The intention was that every venue should have a band, and if the demands of the Musicians' Union had been met, the cost would have been astronomical.)

The thought of a World Cup Opening Ceremony in the presence of Her Majesty the Queen and then the Final without the Massed Bands of the Brigade of Guards was acceptable to no one, least of all to Alec Weeks, who was the BBC producer. It was he who had a brainwave.

He approached Major Jaeger, musical director of the Irish Guards and senior musical director of the Massed Bands of the Brigade of Guards, whom he knew well and with whom he had worked in the past. Jig, as the Major was known to his friends, listened as Alec Weeks told him of the problems.

'Leave it with me,' he told Weeks. Alec Weeks did just that and with the minimum of delay he got the answer. Major Jaeger had taken the problem straight to the Commander-in-Chief of the Brigade of Guards, who had listened carefully and then personally signed the order that the Massed Bands would play at Wembley on the orders of the Commander-in-Chief.

The Commander-in-Chief of the Brigade of Guards is Her Majesty the Queen.

Another problem was solved.

There was another worry as the opening day approached. The Football Association called a full dress rehearsal of the Opening Ceremony for Friday, 8 July. It was such an important rehearsal that someone was engaged to stand in for the Queen. She stood on a podium placed on the track alongside the pitch, just as Her Majesty would the following Monday. In the centre of the pitch were the Massed Bands of the Brigade of Guards, all 200 of them.

On a cue, sixteen groups of youngsters marched out of the tunnel, representing the sixteen finalists. Each group was headed by a Boy Scout carrying the name of the country, and behind him were twenty-two youngsters, dressed in the colours of the country they represented. One of the youngsters carried the national flag.

Now the Football Association might well be among the oldest and most influential associations in the game, and fine administrators of the game of football they may or may not be, depending on your particular point of view. But producers of extravaganzas they certainly were not.

The whole thing was a shambles. The Brigade of Guards, accustomed as they are to excellence, were aghast. Alec Weeks and his counterpart from ITV in the television consortium were looking for an escape route. George Stanton, of Wembley Stadium, was trying to work out how he could go sick the following Monday.

There was a quick conference and it was decided that something had to be done. England's biggest ever sporting event could not be allowed to begin with something right out of *Fawlty Towers*. It just couldn't happen.

It was agreed that George Stanton should approach the Football Association immediately and ask whether Wembley Stadium could take over the production of the Opening Ceremony, or at least the parade part of it. The Football Association, with the sort of alacrity which suggested they were more than delighted to get rid of the responsibility, agreed.

Another quick conference, and inside ten minutes there was agreement between everyone – television, the Massed Bands and Wembley Stadium. It was too late to change anything: all that could be done was to smarten everything and everyone up, because the second run through of the rehearsal, after a tea break, had been an even bigger shambles than the first.

So Jaeger-Stanton Productions took over. First of all, the band was stood down with the exception of the big bass player. Then on to the scene walked a giant of a sergeant-major, whose voice must have resembled claps of thunder for miles around. He took charge of the youngsters as if they were new recruits and worked on them well into the Friday evening until some of them felt fit to drop. They were told to report back to Wembley on the Saturday and again on the Sunday. This really was a case of 'We're going to rehearse this time after time after time after time until we get it one hundred per cent right.'

It was amazing to watch. The only sound came from the deep boom, boom of the bass and the shouted commands of the Sergeant-Major. The lads kept at it, improving ever so slowly, but nevertheless improving. Some were near to tears; some I reckon actually shed tears. They began to find out what blistered feet and aching backs felt like. But it was obvious that there would be no rest until they got it right.

The improvement was easy to see. What had been a stroll became a saunter, then a walk … then a march. No Sergeant-

Major would ever say, 'I think they've got it.' But in the end, this one had to admit that … well, they had got it. A shambles had been turned into a parade.

On the Monday evening, with the Queen, not a stand-in, on the podium, everything was ready. As 200 musicians struck up the music, the Sergeant-Major gave the order to 'March'. The youngsters, now looking the finished article, moved forward under the Sergeant-Major's watchful eye.

Despite the noise of the band, coupled with the rousing cheers of the spectators, the lads could still hear that stentorian voice with its, 'Left, right, left, right … keep those backs straight and those shoulders back.' The Sergeant-Major's discipline had turned them into real stars.

With an hour to go to kick-off I could see the mounting excitement in the spectators' faces as I walked along the track. A policeman greeted me, wished me luck and nodded towards the fans. 'Don't worry,' he said. 'If one single person tries to get over this small wall and on to the pitch, I'll have them.'

At the time I laughed, but later I recalled that the policeman was standing on just about the spot where a few people did get on to the pitch some three hours later!

I had spoken to some of the England players before the start and they were confident. They were confident because they had not been leaking goals – only Portugal had scored against England, and they had some tremendous goalscoring forwards like Eusébio and Torres. Furthermore, England had a settled team. The defence had been in place for some time, and apart from the decision not to play recognized wingmen, only the injury to Greaves had forced a change in the side.

But it was the rock solid defence of England that caused the first flutters of worry. In the thirteenth minute, an error by the normally so dependable Ray Wilson led to Haller giving West Germany the lead. In Ray Wilson's words:

> I shall never forget that first goal. At the start I had been marking Uwe Seeler, the German captain. He was usually at centre forward but had moved to play wide on the right early on in the Final. He was a strong, brave, determined player. Then he changed places with Haller, who wasn't quite as strong or as determined.
>
> So I was a bit casual going for the ball. If I had got it, Haller wouldn't have challenged for it the way Seeler would have done. Yet even though he got possession, Haller didn't hit the ball well, but it struck Big Jack's foot *en route* for goal and we were one down.
>
> The great thing was that we didn't take long to equalize. It was about five minutes and the Germans were slow getting back into position when the referee gave us a free kick. Bobby Moore floated across a gorgeous free kick and Geoff Hurst raced forward and headed it into the net.
>
> From that moment I didn't have the slightest doubt that we would win. If the equalizer had been delayed, the Germans would have grown in confidence, but we ground them down. They played well in the first half but we steamrollered them in the second.

Steamroller them England certainly did and, the longer the second half went on, the more certain it became that England would break the 1–1 deadlock. Alan Ball was an example of perpetual motion, Bobby Moore was majestic and Bobby Charlton was winning his battle with Beckenbauer hands down.

All well and good, but for all the steamrollering, for all the superiority, it was still level at one apiece. That all changed just twelve minutes before the end. England won a corner, the tireless Alan Ball took it, it was cleared, but only towards Geoff Hurst. He shot first time and Schulz tried to hoof it clear. But the ball soared into the air and, as it came down, Martin Peters was there to whack it into the net.

Wembley exploded. England, well on top, were in the lead and the Germans were looking more tired than ever. The England fans' singing of '*When the Reds Go Marching In*' (England wore red in the Final, West Germany white) got louder and louder.

There was little time left when the German launched their death or glory attack. Up from defence came Schulz, Weber and Schnellinger, who had been run ragged by Ball. Seeler appeared to make a back for the much bigger Jack Charlton and the referee's whistle blew, not for an England free kick but for a German one. It was a scratch-your-head-in-disbelief decision.

Ray Wilson saw it that way, too. 'Seeler backed into Big Jack,' he explained, 'and as Jack tried to hold his ground Seeler bent forward. It was he who brought Jack down, not the other way round.'

Referee Dienst would have none of it. He gave West Germany the free kick, Emmerich hit it hard into the goal-mouth where the ball bobbled around for a second or two before Wolfgang Weber forced it over the line. But not, say the English players, before Haller had handled it. Whether he had or not doesn't matter. Mr Dienst gave a goal, West Germany were level.

There were a number of English people not best pleased with that goal. The claim was that the free kick should have been awarded to England, and even after that, Haller had handled before Weber scored.

Over the years, though, I have come to thank the referee for giving the decisions he did, and Wolfgang Weber for scoring that second goal. For just think, if Weber hadn't equalized in the ninetieth minute, England would have won 2–1, there would have been no Geoff Hurst hat-trick, no people on the pitch ... and nobody remembering Kenneth Wolstenholme, and would I not have liked that.

(I told that story at Wembley in 1991 when the Stars Organisation for Spastics held a dinner to celebrate the Silver Jubilee of the World Cup win and as I said, 'My great ambition is to meet Wolfgang Weber again and thank him,' Franz Beckenbauer called out, 'He's just walked in.' He had motored all the way from Cologne just to join in the celebration of a great occasion. We had a long conversation over more than a little red wine, and I just hope he didn't feel as grotty the next morning as I did!)

Extra-time came as a cruel blow for all the players who had given everything during the ninety minutes. Even to think about facing another thirty minutes was sheer hell.

The German players flopped on to the turf; so did some of the England players. Physios raced on to try to massage some life into tired limbs. One man didn't rush on to the pitch. That man was Alf Ramsey. He just strolled on.

The English players were quick to tell him how they felt – knackered. George Cohen was particularly tired because, as he put it:

> I had played thirty-eight games for Fulham during the season on top of the internationals, and near the end of the season I had been in hospital so I had to get fit again, both mentally and physically. And playing at Wembley was a mental strain because the fans always assumed you should do well at home and they'd soon get on your back if you didn't.

Alf didn't dish out sympathy. 'So you're tired,' he told his players. Then, pointing at the Germans: 'What do you think they are? Look at them, they're lying down. Listen, you've won this World Cup once, now get out there and win it again.'

It was a case of forget the tiredness; if you want to be World Champions, act like World Champions. Pull your socks up, tuck your shirts in and win the Cup all over again.

The Germans might well have conceded the match if they'd heard Alf's pick-you-up chat to his team!

The goal everyone still talks about came ten minutes into extra-time. Alan Ball raced down the right to pick up a pass from Stiles. He released the ball inside to Hurst, who let go a shot of frightening ferocity. The ball hit the underside of the round crossbar and even before it had bounced down, the arms of Roger Hunt, who had run to a position almost on the German goal-line, were raised in triumph. So, too, were the arms of English fans standing behind the goal.

Roger Hunt was the major witness in the case which has been argued about these last thirty years. Was it a goal? 'Of course it was,' is Roger's reply.

England went into the second period of extra-time leading 3–2 and determined this time to hold on to the lead. And no one was more determined than Alan Ball, as Nobby Stiles explained on the television programme *Kicking and Screaming*:

Bally was brilliant in that Final. I always remember him running into the back of the net when the goal went in at the end of normal time.

Bally picked up the ball, ran to the centre circle and put it on the spot in the hope that there was enough time for us to make it 3–2. And in extra-time, with about five minutes to go, I was out on my feet. I tried to cross the ball but everything had gone and the ball just trickled over the goal-line. Bally ran past me and said 'Move you little bastard. Keep moving.'

Agonizingly slowly time ticked away. The seconds felt like minutes, the minutes like hours. Right at the death, Bobby Moore won possession deep in England's defensive area. Jack Charlton screamed at him to boot it high into the stand, which is what ninety-nine out of a hundred players would have done. But Bobby was the hundredth. He looked up and saw Geoff Hurst ahead of him.

At that moment, referee Dienst put his whistle in his mouth. I remember thinking, this is it, England have won. It was then that I noticed Moore has chested the ball down in our penalty area and released that perfect pass to Hurst, and that one or two people had climbed over the low wall and were beginning to run on to the pitch. It was then that the words, 'Some people are on the pitch. They think it's all over,' came out. And as Geoff Hurst shot, what else would do but, 'It is now'?

'Some people are on the pitch. They think it's all over. It is now' – fourteen words which have stuck to me ever since. I have even described them as my pension because they have been used so many times by so many people, yet quite honestly I cannot remember ever saying them. But then, the excitement of an occasion can do strange things to the memory ...

Once I was so surprised to be asked whether the words were really off the cuff or whether I had them prepared that I replied, flippantly, that Geoff Hurst and I had rehearsed the whole thing, that Geoff was wearing a deaf aid and could hear my commentary, so knew exactly when to shoot!

For me that was the goal of the match, first because of Bobby Moore's composure and skill in chesting the ball down inside his own penalty area and then delivering such a superb pass to Hurst. Then because of the way Hurst controlled the ball, glanced towards Alan Ball, who was yelling for a square pass to him, and decided on that terrific shot which ended all arguments.

What a great goal to end such a great occasion – England winning the World Cup for the first (and, sadly, still the only) time and Geoff Hurst becoming the first man (and so far the only man) to score a hat-trick in a World Cup Final.

Memories flooded back of the great jubilation, of the way the German supporters cheered England during their lap of honour and of the fact that there was no violence inside or outside the ground.

I had to get down from the commentary position as quickly as possible and make my way to the Interview Room, and it was as I was walking down the tunnel that I saw a lady being escorted by two officials. She saw me, rushed towards me, flung her arms around me and said, with tears in her eyes, 'Kenneth, isn't it wonderful?'

It was wonderful for every English person, but more especially for that lady, Cissie Charlton, mother of Jack and Bobby, a lovely lady steeped in football lore as one would expect from a member of the Milburn family who married into the Charlton family. Sadly, she died just four months before the thirtieth anniversary of her two sons' – and her – greatest moment.

It was pretty late by the time I left the stadium. The crowds had gone, the celebrations had shifted to the route the players' coach was taking to the Royal Garden Hotel for the banquet, and into the West End, where it was VE night all over again.

As I walked to my car I felt as bushed as the players, but I smiled as I saw the empty bottles of champagne littering the car park. Then I heard someone call me.

It was the Secretary of the New Zealand Football
Association asking me to join his party in his car for a glass
of champagne. And he was a Scot by birth, celebrating an
English victory like an Englishman!

One glass and I was homeward bound, my commentating
for the 1966 World Cup finished. My work record read:

July 11 England 0–Uruguay 0 at Wembley
July 12 Brazil 2–Bulgaria 0 at Goodison Park
July 13 Portugal 3–Hungary 1 at Old Trafford
July 15 Hungary 3–Brazil 1 at Goodison Park
July 16 England 2–Mexico 0 at Wembley
July 19 Uruguay 0–Mexico 0 at Wembley
July 23 England 1–Argentina 0 Quarter-final at Wembley
July 25 West Germany 2–Russia 1 Quarter-final at Goodi-
    son Park
July 26 England 2–Portugal 1 Semi-final at Wembley
July 28 Portugal 2–Russia 1 3rd and 4th Place Playoff at
    Wembley
July 30 England 4–West Germany 2 Final at Wembley

As I drove along the North Circular road, through Richmond
and Kingston to my Surrey home for an early night, I thought
to myself that they could feel doubtful about the legality of
England's third goal if they wished, but there was a far
stronger case for feeling doubtful about the West German
second, on two counts. But then if that goal had been disallowed there would have been no people on the pitch.

Perhaps the greatest moment of the whole day, though,
was when Alf Ramsey was approached by one of his critics
who said to him, 'Well done, Alf. I always knew you'd do it.'

He got the deserved answer: a straight face and 'That's not
what you said before the competition.'

9

Was It In Or Wasn't It?

For a forty-five-year-old Swiss gentleman from Basle, 30 July 1966 was the greatest day of his life. It was the day he realized the ambition of every football referee – he refereed the World Cup Final.

That man was Gottfried Dienst. He began as a player with FC Basle in the Swiss First Division, but was forced into early retirement because of a knee injury. He took up refereeing and in no time at all was on the FIFA list. Mr Dienst was entrusted with many big games, starting with the 1961 European Cup Final in Berne between Barcelona and Benfica. (Benfica won 3–2 and took the trophy away from Spain for the first time. The previous Finals in 1956, 1957, 1958, 1959 and 1960 had all been won by the most talented team of those days, Real Madrid.) He also refereed the 1965 Final in which Inter Milan beat Benfica 1–0 in Milan's San Siro Stadium.

He was an official of vast experience and was well aware that football matches, like all sporting events, can provide controversy, but little did he realize that he would become the central figure in a controversy which would rumble on and on and still not be resolved after thirty years.

131

There have been plenty of dubious decisions made by referees in World Cup matches. Who can forget Diego 'The Hand of God' Maradona? Did he handle the ball into the net as the television cameras seemed to suggest, or was the referee correct in deciding he had used his head to score a fair goal for Argentina against England in the 1986 World Cup?

Was Jack Taylor, that splendid referee from Wolverhampton, right or was he too harsh in awarding Holland a penalty kick in the very first minute of the 1974 Final against West Germany in Munich? Some may argue he was wrong, but no one can doubt his courage. (For the record, although Holland scored from the penalty kick, the Germans went on to win the Cup 2–1.)

Then what about Clive Thomas, the Welsh referee from Treorchy? The Brazilians certainly remember him. Mr Thomas awarded Brazil a corner kick in a 1978 World Cup match against Sweden and from the corner the ball was headed into the net for what seemed a legitimate goal. But Mr Thomas had blown his whistle to signify the end of the forty-five minutes as the ball was *en route* from the corner flag to a lethal Brazilian head. No goal!

The more cynical citizens of the world – and that included the whole of Brazil! – wondered whether referees had watches good enough to keep time to the split second, but the fact remains that the referee is the only judge of time and when, in his opinion, forty-five minutes, plus any stoppage time, have elapsed, he has to blow his whistle. In Clive Thomas's case it was hard on Brazil, but no harder than the referee blowing his whistle when a forward is bearing down on the opposing goal with only the goalkeeper to beat.

The controversy which followed Clive Thomas's and Jack Taylor's decisions and Maradona's disputed goal was a nothing compared with the hoo-hah which followed Mr

Dienst's validation of England's third goal in the 1966 World Cup Final. The teams were locked at two-all in the first half of extra-time when Alan Ball slipped a pass inside to Geoff Hurst. Perhaps it wasn't the greatest of passes insofar as the ball was slightly behind Hurst, who had to turn to get in his shot. But turn he did and he hit it well. The ball rattled the underside of the rounded crossbar, bounced down and English arms went up claiming a goal.

From my commentary position high up on the gantry and level with the centre line it was impossible for me to tell whether it was a goal or not. Three things, though, suggested to me that it was. First, Bobby Charlton – and you couldn't meet a fairer sportsman – began to celebrate. Second, the crowd behind the goal raised their arms almost to a man, and I have since spoken to a man who was standing there (at the cost of £1.75, or £1.17s.6d. as it was in those days) and he told me that there was no doubt in his mind that it was a goal).

But the clinching evidence is provided by Roger Hunt. Like the excellent predator he was, he came running towards the German goal and was almost on the goal-line when the ball struck the bar. He immediately flung up his arms, turned and ran to congratulate Hurst. Later on I asked him why he hadn't kicked the ball into the back of the net to save any argument, and he replied: 'Because I had already seen the ball swerve well over the line.'

Hunt was such a goalscorer that he would have loved nothing more than to have been credited with a World Cup Final goal, especially a goal which looked as if it was going to be the winning one. So it is inconceivable that he would throw up that chance unless he was a hundred per cent certain Hurst's shot had been over the line.

Mr Dienst's version of the incident is an honest one. He admits he was in no position to know whether the ball had crossed the line, so he consulted his linesman, a Russian by the name of Tofik Bahkramov. He indicated that a goal was the correct decision so Mr Dienst had no hesitation in pointing to the centre spot, pursued as he was by three protesting German players. To the eternal credit of the German team, the protests soon fizzled out under orders from the captain, Uwe Seeler, who pulled away the players who were chasing the referee.

I couldn't help smiling as I pointed out in my commentary that, according to the FIFA handout given to all members of the media, Mr Dienst spoke English, French, German and Italian. Mr Bahkramov spoke Russian and Turkish. There was no common language between them except the language of football.

Thirty years on people still ask, 'Was it a goal?' All the reference books tell us that it was. But a good friend of mine, Philip Differ, an excellent writer and producer of comedy shows for the BBC in Glasgow, has always claimed that Geoff Hurst is the only man to be credited with a hat-trick for scoring only two goals. But then as a true Scot he would, wouldn't he?

The arguments will rage on for as long as anyone who saw the 1966 Final at Wembley or on television is drawing breath. The Germans have produced countless photographs which show the ball bouncing on the line when ALL the ball must be over the line for the goal to count. But camera angles can often be misleading.

A couple of computer buffs sought to produce computerized evidence that the ball didn't cross the line but merely bounced on it. Their evidence was flawed because, for a vital second or two, the ball is hidden behind the goalkeeper. 'But,' said the scientists, 'we can assume that the ball ...' Any footballer could tell them that you can never assume what a football will do (or has done).

Wembley have an amusing exhibit in their Great Hall. It is a mock-up of a goal with the ball beating the goalkeeper and striking the crossbar, which, incidentally, is the actual crossbar that was used on the big day. To one side is a television replay of the incident at normal speed and then in slow motion.

Visitors are asked to press the blue button if they think it was a goal and to press the red button if they think it wasn't. Naturally enough, the English visitors press the blue button while the Germans (and Philip Differ!) press the red.

But despite the computers, the cameras and Wembley's amusing mock-up, which gives much pleasure to those who go on the Wembley tour, the fact remains that the referee's decision is final and there is little or no point in arguing thirty years after the event.

Perhaps the error many people make is watching where the ball lands. They fail to notice that after the ball struck the crossbar, it swerved well over the line in mid-air, as Roger Hunt has said so many times. And if the ball is over the line in mid-air the decision must be a goal, irrespective of where the ball lands, as a German television crew discovered in 1995.

They challenged Geoff Hurst to repeat his shot to see whether he could swerve the ball into the net. Obliging gentleman that he is, Geoff turned up on Sunday morning and shot six times from the same spot the television crew reckoned he had shot from in 1966. Six times the ball hit the underside of the crossbar and six times the ball spun over the line before bouncing down on or near to it.

Exit in haste a very embarrassed television crew, while Geoff Hurst went home to enjoy his Sunday lunch.

All the same Messrs Dienst, now seventy-six and living in Basle, and Bahkramov, who died aged sixty-six in 1993, just a month after Bobby Moore, will always be remembered as the two officials at the centre of one of football's biggest controversies.

10

The Genius Behind the Triumph

As the England team took the field at Wembley after the Opening Ceremony in July 1966, the majority of the nation did not share Alf Ramsey's optimistic view that we were on the brink of a memorable victory.

The fact that almost everybody was going round just after five o'clock on the afternoon of 30 July saying 'I told you so', only proves that some people had undergone a conversion comparable to that of St Paul on the road to Damascus.

But Alf Ramsey, never a man to suffer fools gladly, just smiled. He was willing to be judged by his record.

Alfred Ernest Ramsey was a Londoner, born the son of a grocer in Dagenham, and before anyone cries that Dagenham is in Essex, not London, let me point out that in the past Dagenham lads were chosen to play for London schools.

Two other illustrious football figures – Jimmy Greaves and Terry Venables – shared Alf Ramsey's town honours. Just consider the three careers:

	GREAVES	RAMSEY	VENABLES
Born	East Ham	Dagenham	Dagenham
Town honours	Dagenham Schools	Dagenham Schools	Dagenham Schools
Area honours	London Schools		London Schools
County	Essex Schools	Essex Schools	
Pro career	Chelsea	Southampton	Chelsea
	AC Milan	Spurs	Spurs
	Spurs		QPR
	West Ham United		
International	England Youth	England B	England Schools
	England Under-23	England	England Amateur
	England		England Youth
			England Under-23
			England
Manager England	No	Yes	Yes
Manager/Coach	No	Yes	Yes

All in all, Dagenham, Essex and Spurs have a lot to be proud of.

Alf Ramsey was born on 22 January 1920 so was only nineteen when the Second World War broke out. Portsmouth were the first club to show interest in him and he signed amateur forms for them in 1940. But his senior career got off to a stuttering start due to the war, so that was the last he heard from Portsmouth, where folk then had a little more on their mind than football.

Called up into the Army, Alf played for his battalion which was based in Hampshire. One of the games in which he took part was against Southampton. He was at centre half, and Southampton won 10–1! Despite that heavy defeat, young Ramsey must have made an impression because, after playing in an Army side which beat Southampton's reserve side, he was signed by the Saints as an amateur. He later signed as a professional and changed position from centre half to right back, a wise decision because just after the war he began to win representative honours. First he played for England B and then for the Football League. In December 1948 he won the first of his thirty-two full England caps when he was selected to play against Switzerland.

His stylish full-back play had by now made him a household name, so it was no surprise that at the end of the 1948–49 season he joined Tottenham Hotspur for £21,000, which was then a record transfer fee for a full back. Ramsey became a member of the Tottenham push-and-run side fashioned by manager Arthur Rowe, a side many people believe was the finest ever to represent the club.

An important part of the Spurs push-and-run style, with its accent on elegant, entertaining football, was the build-up of attacks from the back – the very back. Arthur Rowe liked his goalkeeper, Ted Ditchburn, to throw rather than kick the ball clear, and with Alf Ramsey, a calm, unflappable full back who was an immaculate passer of the ball, it was easy to see how the cultured Tottenham style developed. It took Tottenham to the Second Division Championship in 1950, and the following season the First Division felt the full might of Spurs, who raced away to their second successive title.

Even then Alf Ramsey was showing signs of being a clever tactician, and this was why he was made club captain when Ronnie Burgess, the brilliant Welsh international, left.

More and more international honours came his way; in fact he made twenty-eight consecutive appearances for England, thirty-two appearances altogether, and he was involved in the 1950 World Cup and England's 1953 games against the Rest of the World and Hungary.

The first time England entered the World Cup was in 1950 and few people realized the class of the opposition they would meet in Brazil. But England's humiliation came at the hands of one of the minnows of the game – the United States of America.

England lost to the United States by the only goal of the match in Belo Horizonte, a result which shocked the world, let alone England. In fact, it caused such a sensation in America that the *New York Times*, fearing an error, refused to print the score. And just in case you think England fielded a weakened side in the match, cast your eyes on this line-up: Bert Williams (Wolves); Alf Ramsey (Tottenham Hotspur), John Aston (Manchester United); Billy Wright (Wolves), captain, Laurie Hughes (Liverpool), Jimmy Dickinson (Portsmouth); Tom Finney (Preston North End), Stanley Mortensen (Blackpool), Roy Bentley (Chelsea), Wilf Mannion (Middlesbrough), Jimmy Mullen (Wolves).

The Rest of the World team we had been expecting at Wembley on 21 October 1953 turned out to be a Rest of Europe team, and because the all-conquering Hungarians were due to visit Wembley five weeks later, there were no Hungarians in the line-up. All the same it was a formidable eleven England faced and England looked to be going down to a 4–3 defeat until the referee awarded a debatable penalty near the end. Up stepped Alf Ramsey, the penalty taker in chief, and it ended four each.

There was no such escape five weeks later when the Hungarians murdered England 6–3, but once again Alf Ramsey converted a penalty. That match, which was the first and last time both Ernie Taylor and George Robb played for England, ended Alf's illustrious international career, and it was also the end of the road for Bill Eckersley, Harry Johnston and Jackie Sewell.

One international disaster decimated more than half of the England team, with six players bidding farewell to the international scene. A disaster *par excellence..*

But not such a disaster for Alf Ramsey because he was nearing the end of his fine career as a player, and at the beginning of the 1955–56 season, at the age of thirty-five, he decided to hang up his boots and accept the manager's job at Ipswich Town.

Ipswich were an old-established club, having been formed in 1880, but they didn't turn professional until 1936. The club was originally called Ipswich Association Football Club to distinguish it from the older Ipswich Football Club, which played rugby. The clubs amalgamated in 1888, and five years later it was decided to concentrate on Association Football.

The first President of the club was the MP, Mr T. C. Cobbold, and to this day the Cobbold family is represented on the Ipswich Town Board of Directors. When Alf Ramsey became manager, the President was Lady Blanche Cobbold, the Chairman was John Cobbold, and today's President, Mr P. Cobbold was also on the Board.

The Cobbolds were a local brewery family and they believed in running a friendly, happy club. They would invite a guest into the Boardroom after a match, pour him or her a drink and then, especially when the late John Cobbold was Chairman, explain, 'This is the last drink you'll be given. Here we're a happy family so we all serve ourselves. So do help yourself.'

Many a time did I travel home by train with the team after a match when they amused themselves by everyone, players and directors alike, thinking up limericks about the opposing club, its players or even its officials.

Then there was the lovely story the late Ted Croker told when he was Secretary of the Football Association. In 1978,

long after Alf Ramsey had left the club, Ipswich Town got to
the FA Cup Final. Before the official lunch which precedes
the game, Lady Cobbold was asked by Ted Croker whether
she would like to meet Prime Minister Harold Wilson. 'If it's
all the same to you,' she replied, 'I'd rather have a large gin
and tonic.'

When Alf Ramsey took over at Ipswich Town they had just
been relegated back to Division Three (South) after just one
season in the Second Division.

Alf was to change all that, and soon. In his second season
with them he took them to third spot, but that wasn't good
enough for promotion. The following season was, though.
They finished as Champions in 1956–57, albeit just edging
out Torquay United on goal average (as it was then). In
1960–61 they finished on top of the Second Division and for
the first time in the club's history they were in the First
Division.

There were greater things to come. Alf Ramsey had got
together such a fine squad that Ipswich shot to the top of the
First Division and stayed there, finishing three points ahead of
Burnley (in the days of just two points for a win) with Spurs,
the Cup winners that season, another point behind. In just
seven seasons, Alf had taken Ipswich Town from the pits of
the Third Division to the very pinnacle of the First Division.

Alf had flummoxed the First Division with some original
thinking. He relied a great deal on his two main strikers, Ray
Crawford and Ted Phillips. Between them this formidable
duo scored sixty-one goals in the Championship season.
Crawford was capped twice that year – against Northern
Ireland and Austria – and, though he scored against Austria,
that was to be the sum total of his international appearances.
Ted Phillips was never capped and many, perhaps most,

people were mystified as to why they were never chosen in tandem because it was their uncanny partnership that brought out the best in both of them at Ipswich.

But Ipswich were not a two-man team. It was just that Alf used his two strikers cleverly. They were both good finishers and they were both mobile. They could draw defenders out of position and create space for their colleagues. The two wingmen, Stephenson and Leadbetter, were played deep, giving Ipswich a 4–4–2 formation, although nobody liked to talk in numbers in those days.

George Cohen tells of seeing the system in its infancy:

We gave Ipswich a real thrashing at Craven Cottage, but the return game was at Portman Road a few weeks later and what a change there was. In no time at all they were two goals up and we were looking around trying to find their players. With the wingmen so withdrawn, I don't think I got within twenty-five yards of Jimmy Lead-better all afternoon, and eventually they won 4–2.

But that was Alf Ramsey all over. He was a thinker about the game and he made full use of the talent at his disposal.

After winning the Championship, Ipswich had to meet the FA Cup winners in the annual Charity Shield fixture, so it was Spurs who provided the opposition at Portman Road on 11 August 1962.

And though Alf had an astute footballing brain, Spurs possessed a couple of wily thinkers of their own in their manager, Bill Nicholson, and their captain, Danny Blanch-flower. So Spurs had done their homework and went to Portman Road knowing all about the withdrawn wingmen and the double threat of Crawford and Phillips. Maurice

Norman and Dave Mackay took care of the Ipswich strikers and the Spurs full backs abandoned their usual role of marking the wingmen so that they were not drawn out of position. The result was that Spurs trumped the Ipswich ace and won by five goals to one.

As First Division Champions Ipswich were, of course, in Europe that season and in the Preliminary Round they were drawn against Floriana, of Malta. It was a hilarious trip to the Mediterranean island and Ipswich did a marvellous job on a pitch of baked clay covered with sand. They won 4–1 with a couple of goals each for Crawford and Phillips. The second leg was one-way traffic and Ipswich won 10–1, Ray Crawford scoring five.

Ipswich had gone just over halfway through their season as Champions when the bitter blow fell. In January 1963 Alf Ramsey was invited to become England manager. He accepted.

The Ipswich team were training when Alf Ramsey ordered them into the dressing-room, where he told them the news. The players were delighted for the Boss, but sad for themselves because Alf Ramsey was a popular manager and the players knew they owed him everything. Meanwhile, the Chairman of the club, John Cobbold, was in tears. He thought the world of Alf and knew that England's gain was Ipswich's loss.

We know now what a gain it was for England. Three and a half years after he was appointed he had built a squad capable of making England the World Champions. What is more, he wasn't far away from doing it a second time in Mexico in 1970.

He did his homework about conditions in Mexico and made sure that on the 1969 tour the team played in

Guadalajara, where, as holders, England would play the first round a year later. I remember asking him in the Hilton Hotel there where the team would be staying in 1970 and he answered, 'Right here in the Hilton.' I pressed him further, 'You mean the entire party, officials as well?'

Alf gave me that you-should-know-better look of his and said simply, 'The players will be here, so will I and my team. I don't know where the officials will be staying. They are nothing to do with me.'

Many people think that the squad he took to Mexico was better than the one he had in 1966. England qualified for the quarter-finals in second place, beating Rumania and Czechoslovakia both by 1–0, and losing by the same score in a splendid match against Brazil.

The wheels came off for England in the quarter-final at Leon against West Germany – yes, West Germany again. England had a blow before the game when Gordon Banks was found to be unfit, but early in the second half the World Champions were two goals to the good. However, later in the second half, during which Alf Ramsey made two strange substitutions, the Germans equalized, and in extra-time they scored the winner.

Many were the recriminations. Why, for instance, had Ramsey taken off Bobby Charlton when England were 2–1 up and replaced him with Colin Bell? Then why had Peters been replaced by Norman Hunter with ten minutes to go? Many people thought the substitutions were made because England looked safe and players needed resting for the semi-final and, maybe, the Final. But two minutes after Peters left the field, West Germany scored the equalizer. They were now on a high, while English heads dropped, and extra-time produced the killing blow – a third German goal. England were out.

This meant climbing the Everest of the qualifying competition for the 1974 World Cup. It was an Everest England failed to climb. Sir Alf Ramsey, the man who had brought pride to English football, was shown the door. Knighted in 1966, sacked in May 1974. Football fame is fleeting, even when you have a knighthood.

There were those who said Alf was not a good PR man, but on every tour I went with a Ramsey-led team he was scrupulously fair. He made it quite clear that he would give no exclusive interviews. Everyone, no matter which newspaper, television company or radio station they were employed by would be treated the same way.

He realized that he couldn't satisfy all the members of the media with the timing of his team selections. So he handed the job over to the media! He knew that if a game was on a Sunday, the team announcement should be made in time for the Sunday newspaper reporters to get it into their newspapers. The team selections for the other games would be divided between the morning and evening newspapers. He knew the press had a job to do and he helped them do it whenever he could.

There wasn't an ounce of flamboyance in either Alf the player or Alf the manager. Some people called him taciturn, and perhaps he was at times, but he would never have been the success he was if he had been uncooperative or withdrawn.

He showed his true colours at the end of the World Cup Final. Surrounded by scenes of jubilation the like of which even Wembley had never witnessed, he stood calmly outside the touchline, his face completely devoid of emotion. While others cheered and danced, the architect of the victory stood motionless.

When the time came for Bobby Moore to lead his team up to the Royal Box for the presentation, Alf Ramsey stepped forward, held his hand out to Bobby Moore, his captain, and then proceeded to shake the hand of each of his players as they walked past him.

That was Alf Ramsey. He had been determined to win. He had been confident his team would win. The job had been done.

Sir Alf Ramsey was disgusted at the decision to sack him:

> I said we would win the World Cup the day I took the job and I never changed my opinion. I always told my players that they had to accept the fact that if we were to win the World Cup, my job was to do my work well, their job was to do their work well. I think we all succeeded.
>
> Then I was sacked and it hurt. It still does.

But Sir Alf was a proud man, a man who cherished the dual honour of being an England player and an England manager. The sack wounded him deeply, but it didn't make him lose his dignity.

Sir Alf Ramsey was dignified in defeat, as in that first game in Paris. He was dignified in victory, as on 30 July 1966. And he was dignified in disappointment, as on the day he was sacked.

He had lasted in the England job for more than eleven years. He was succeeded by Don Revie (three years), Ron Greenwood (five years), Bobby Robson (eight years) and Graham Taylor (three and a half years).

The record of the five managers who succeeded Sir Walter Winterbottom and preceded Terry Venables is:

	Played	Won	Drawn	Lost	Points	Percentage
Sir Alf Ramsey	113	69	27	17	234	69.03
Ron Greenwood	55	33	12	10	111	67.27
Bobby Robson	95	47	30	18	171	60.00
Graham Taylor	37	17	13	7	64	57.66
Don Revie	29	14	8	7	50	57.47

(*Note*: The modern system of three points for a win has been used.)

11

Sir Alf ... By the Lads

Asking the members of the 1966 squad what Alf Ramsey was like is somewhat akin to compiling a dossier for the Sir Alf Ramsey's Fan Club magazine. Nevertheless, everyone else has had their say about Sir Alf – the officials, the media and the fans – so it is only fair to allow the players, who served under him in the toughest of all competitions, to have theirs.

Alan Ball

Alf was the greatest. He was the model for all managers. Some managers are good at tactics, some are good at coaching and some are good at motivation and man management. Alf was one hundred per cent at all three. You can't say that about many managers.

He was always fair, always honest and above all he was always loyal. Look at the way he supported Nobby Stiles when people were howling for him to be dropped because of one mistimed tackle. The loyalty that Alf showed to all his players was repaid by loyalty and honesty.

He never wasted words. He was always straight and to the point.

Gerry Byrne

A wonderful manager, the best. He built a real team with real team spirit.

Geoff Hurst

What can you say about the man who was the very best? You always knew where you stood with him. If you played badly he would tell you so. If you played well he'd tell you that, as well. But he'd never overdo the praise. He always wanted his players to feel that they were part of a team, but he never wanted anyone to think they were indispensable. When we were dispersing after one international, a player said to Alf, 'Cheerio, boss. See you next time.' Alf just looked at him and replied, 'Are you sure?'

That was Alf's way. He liked to joke a little, to tease a little but he always wanted the players to realize that there was no divine right to their selection.

His substitutions in 1970 were a mistake, but who never made a mistake?

Martin Peters

Alf deserves all the accolades he has received. He was the very best of managers, a player's man through and through. If you gave of your best to him he would never forget you, but he had no time for the slackers.

He had an unrivalled knowledge of the game and he could communicate that knowledge to the players. He didn't produce long, complicated dossiers on opponents. He kept his instructions simple.

He once said I was ten years ahead of my time. People often asked me what that meant. I was never sure. But I bet Alf was.

Peter Bonetti

It was a great joy to be in the squad and to experience such camaraderie, which was all down to the manager. He made every one of the twenty-two squad members feel important, and the supreme confidence that he had in his forecast that we would win the World Cup did wonders for the team. Managers are infectious. If they have doubts, those doubts are transmitted to the players. Alf never had any doubts. He knew the players he wanted and he picked them.

Just being part of the squad really did inflate the old ego. You felt ten feet tall, and although it was obvious that I was the third-choice goalkeeper, I still felt proud to be part of it all. That is the spirit Sir Alf Ramsey instilled into those he had chosen.

Ron Springett

I had, and still have, the utmost respect for Sir Alf Ramsey. He was the sort of manager every player would love to serve. During the run-up to the World Cup matches we trained at the Bank of England Club at Roehampton. Jimmy Greaves asked Alf if we could nip home for a day, but Alf refused. 'We are a team,' he said, 'and we are going to stay as a team.'

I pointed out that I lived no more than fifty yards from the Bank of England Club, so, one day after a training session, Alf said, 'You can go home for a cup of tea.'

I took him up on his offer, but, knowing Alf, I didn't stay longer than it takes to drink a cup of tea.

When I got back to the Bank of England Club, the first shot that came my way went right through my legs into the net.

'That's the last time I let you nip home for a cup of tea, Ron,' was all Alf said.

He was a super guy. No one could wish to have a better manager. He knew exactly what he wanted from his players and he chose the players who would give him what he wanted. You always knew exactly where you stood with him.

He didn't have favourites ... nobody got any special favours. We were all part of a team, and Alf never got tired of telling us, 'Look, I've got my job to do and you've got yours. If I do my job well and you do your job well, the World Cup will be ours.'

Gordon Banks

I have all the admiration in the world for Sir Alf Ramsey. He was the sort of man who could ease out just a little bit more from even the world's greatest player.

He never let us grow over-confident, which was a good thing because we all knew the strength of the opposition. So, too, did Alf. He knew the sort of game countries would play against us because he had done his homework.

Over-confident we weren't; confident we were. We had only lost two and drawn three of seventeen internationals from the beginning of 1965 to the first match of the World Cup. I had played in all but two of those games. So we were on a high and really believed we could do it.

We had been briefed to the nth degree by Alf. He told us that Uruguay would, especially in the first match, the show match following the Opening Ceremony, do everything in their power to crowd their own penalty area. They would try to frustrate us by their blanket defence, and they would happily settle for a draw (which they got) but hope that they might snatch a goal on the break (which they didn't).

Alf was alive to all those plans and he reckoned that we had the players capable of finding a way round any tactics the opposition might employ. He had confidence in us, and we had confidence in him.

Norman Hunter

First, second, third and last, Alf Ramsey was a player's man. He had been a great player himself and knew exactly how a player thinks. He studied the men he chose. He knew those who needed the odd gee-up, those who needed the gentle treatment, those who needed the come-on-get-up-and-go treatment. He was well aware that no two players are alike, but he studied his men as an Army commander does and treated them accordingly.

So many people thought him austere and uncommunicative. That was the general opinion of him held by the public, by some members of the media and even by some of the Football Association officials. But nothing could be further from the truth.

He was an absolute gentleman, and a caring gentleman at that. True, he was a demanding gentleman, but all managers have to be if they want to be great. Alf didn't just want to be great, he was determined to be great. And he was great.

There were times when he showed a lovely sense of humour. He once gave us a week-end off and described that as 'a bit of remission for good behaviour.'

Jimmy Armfield

I was the senior pro in the World Cup squad, although I suppose Ron Flowers ran me pretty close. I had been in the game a long time, I had seen many changes, and I had studied many managers. And where would I place Alf Ramsey? Right at the very top. There have only been a few really great managers in the game, and Alf Ramsey was one of them, both with Ipswich Town and with England.

Managing a national side is no easy job. In fact it's a thankless job. Unlike a club manager, a national team manager doesn't have the players on a day-to-day basis. In fact, he sees them very rarely, and it was much worse in 1966 than it is today.

Not having the players with him every day means that a national team manager cannot get the player playing to his orders all the time, simply because his club might play a different system to the one favoured by the national team. Alf was fully aware of this and he knew that he had to be careful to select the right players, and by that I don't mean necessarily the best players in the country. He had to select the players who would do the right job at the right time, players who would realize that their club style might differ from the national style. In other words, players who were versatile.

For instance, I am sure that there were some people who wouldn't have chosen either Alan Ball or Roger Hunt for the World Cup squad, but Alf knew that to win the World Cup would be a long, hard graft. There are players who are very skilful but, when the chips are down, cannot graft. They are not much good in a crisis. Alan and Roger could play and they could graft. That made them vital to the World Cup squad.

Alf knew that, which is why he deserved to succeed. He also had the great knack of spotting the player who, given the opportunity, would emerge as a star.

At the start of the World Cup we were well served in the goal-scoring department. Roger Hunt was a great scorer. He had proved himself for Liverpool and for England. With Jimmy Greaves alongside him it seemed certain England could score against the best. Then there was Bobby Charlton. Who could ask for more?

Alf Ramsey, that's who. He had spotted a striker who was bursting with talent and decided to blood him on the international scene early in 1966. He did enough to earn a place in the squad. I'm referring to Geoff Hurst, and what a prize he turned out to be.

And because he had the knack of finding players like Geoff Hurst and getting the best out of them, I rate Sir Alf Ramsey as the best and most complete manager England has ever had.

Ron Flowers

When the telephone rang and the voice at the other end said, 'This is Alf Ramsey here. Just to let you know, Ron, that I've chosen you in the twenty-two for the World Cup,' I could have jumped over the moon. I'd had a long run in the England side, but I thought my international days were over, so it was a great bonus for me. Just wonderful.

Alf was simply magnificent. I say that not because he chose me, but because he was magnificent in everything he did. He was painstaking. Nothing escaped his notice, and if you look at the sides he chose from that game against France in Paris onwards, you could see the World Cup team developing. Some players fell by the wayside because they couldn't live up to the high standards Alf set, but slowly and surely Alf put together all the pieces into the right places in the jigsaw puzzle.

I learned a lot from Alf. I wish I'd known what he taught me ten years earlier. That's how good he was. He knew the game backwards.

Like everyone else on the pre-World Cup tour, I got a game – you can call it the easy one – against Norway, if you like. When we had finished in Scandinavia and headed for Poland, I reckon Alf knew his first eleven for the World Cup. It was the team he chose to beat the Poles: Gordon Banks; George Cohen, Jack Charlton, Bobby Moore, Ray Wilson; Alan Ball, Nobby Stiles, Bobby Charlton, Martin Peters; Jimmy Greaves, Roger Hunt. Sounds familiar, doesn't it?

I sat next to Jimmy Armfield watching that game and I said to him, 'Jim, I can't see anyone beating this team.'

Nobody did, not even after the enforced change of Geoff Hurst for the injured Jimmy Greaves.

Yes, Alf Ramsey was a genius among managers. Nobody should ever forget what he did for English football.

Ian Callaghan

We had six weeks together before the World Cup started. Some of the time we were at Lilleshall, the rest of the time on tour to Scandinavia and Poland. During that time we developed a team spirit second to none. There were no bad apples in the barrel, no moaners and groaners, no trouble-makers. And it was all down to Alf Ramsey.

He was a real player's manager. He didn't mollycoddle anyone, but he always insisted that the players came first. He made the decisions and every member of the squad accepted them. It wasn't easy, believe me, when you find out that the boss has dropped you from the team, but you have to take it because time and time again Alf made decisions which turned out to be the right ones.

He was his own man. Once he made his mind up, that was it, and no amount of criticism would make him change his mind. It didn't matter who was making the criticism – offi-cials, press, public. All were ignored. Alf Ramsey was the manager, the boss, the man who was willing to stand or fall by his own ability and by the ability of the players in whom he had placed his faith.

Yes, a terrific manager and one I am proud to have served.

John Connelly

One hundred per cent, ten out of ten, and if you can think of any other way of giving someone full marks, well and good. That's what I think of Alf Ramsey. He didn't pick me for the Final. I wish he had, but he did what he thought was right, and Alf was almost always uncannily right.

He was a brilliant manager. It was he who fostered such a spirit among the lads, and he made sure that being in the squad was just like being in a club. He was out on his own when it came to man management.

He knew every one of his players inside out, their strengths and their weaknesses. What is more, he knew exactly how to get the best out of his players. Alf never took anything for granted. He believed you never got anything without working for it.

I've heard it said that he was sometimes a bit aloof with the lads. Maybe he was, but you knew that he would never let you down. All of us respected him. We'd run through a brick wall for him.

He was a brilliant tactician and he wasn't afraid to experiment. He was such a brave manager, determined in his team selection and then determined to make his selection work. A former international player himself, he knew that everyone had to be relaxed before a big game, so he would always tell a player in good time that he was going to play. He never left anyone in limbo wondering whether he was in the team or not.

I'm still full of admiration for him and for the life of me I cannot understand why on earth he was sacked. Despite the disappointment of failing to qualify for the 1974 World Cup, Alf would have pulled our game round. With him in charge we would never have dropped to twenty-something in the international ratings.

Believe me, Sir Alf Ramsey has forgotten more about football and man management than his critics have ever known.

Jimmy Greaves

He was a great manager and those people who say we had arguments are talking a lot of old rubbish.

All that talk was invented when I didn't play in the Final, but all the stories about me being dropped were nonsense. I wasn't fit. I knew it and Alf knew it, and Alf was too good a manager to consider choosing an unfit player.

I've always got on well with Alf. I have always respected him as a man and as a manager. He was very single-minded. He wanted to get the right squad from which he could choose the right team to win the World Cup in 1966. He set out to do it, and he did it. Not only that, he did it in the proper manner.

You can't ask any more of any man.

George Cohen

There's just one word to describe him: wonderful. He treated everyone as a man and expected everyone to behave as a man. He was always consistent in his behaviour and in his attitude towards us players. He didn't overload us with tactics talks. He picked his men on their club form and expected them to reproduce their club form for England. But you had to fit in with his plan for England.

Alf was a very thorough man. He was his own man, but he never behaved like a know-all. Far from it. He was always ready and willing to listen to any ideas the players had, and if one of them appealed to him he would consider it and then say, 'Well, let's give it a try.' If he didn't like it, then nothing more would be heard about it.

He used Harold Shepherdson, the chief trainer and unofficial assistant manager, to keep him informed as to what the players were thinking and how they were feeling.

There was one occasion when we were in Copenhagen and most of us felt a bit bored being stuck in the hotel during the evening. Harold Shepherdson got wind of this, dropped a hint to Alf, and when Alf asked him, 'Do you think the lads would like to go out tonight?', Shep was quick to answer, 'Yes, I think they would.' Alf agreed and we went out.

He never treated us like children, but he was quick to show anyone who stepped out of line who was the boss. Yet he would hand out reprimands as he did everything – calmly, quietly and only after careful consideration. He never lost his temper, never even raised his voice, but he always made his point. He expected – and got – discipline because there was always mutual respect between players and manager. Which is how it should be.

I remember once when we were going off on an overseas tour, on the eve of our departure five of the party slipped out of the hotel without permission. Alf found out who the culprits were and carefully placed their passports on their beds. No note, no anything. Just the passport.

The next morning, before we left for the airport, Alf had a quiet word with the whole squad. All he said was, 'Five of you found your passports on your beds. You know why and you know that if there had been time to call up five other players to replace you I would have done so.'

That's all. He didn't mention any names, but his message had got home.

Yes, Alf Ramsey was a real professional who knew football and footballers backwards. Yet the Football Association didn't realize what a gem they had.

It was stupid of them to sack him, absolutely scandalous. They should have let him take on an assistant he could groom as his successor. In that way we would have had continuity.

But what happened? Alf was thrown out, we lost that continuity and we have never regained it. We were going nowhere until Alf was appointed manager, and we've been going nowhere since he was sacked. Those who seek the answer to the question, 'What has happened to our football?' need look no further than the day Sir Alf Ramsey was thrown on to the scrapheap by the Football Association.

Ray Wilson

Alf had a bad start to his career as England's manager – that 5–2 defeat by France in Paris. But he soon began to mould a good side together. Our morale went higher and higher, but frankly I never thought of our winning the World Cup.

It was vital for us to win our group once the final stages began, and we were thankful that we were not in a very strong group. I couldn't see anyone giving us a great deal of trouble except France. Many people said that we had a big advantage playing all our games at Wembley, but I'm not so sure of that. The home fans in London are very critical and that puts more and more pressure on the players. We are seeing it happening today.

Once we were through our first-round group, I thought we had a good chance of reaching at least the semi-final. I think that is the most many of the players thought we would get.

But Alf never harboured any thought like that. He said at the very start of his reign that he would win the World Cup, and win the World Cup he was determined to do. And his genius and thoroughness stood out when we played Portugal in the semi-final, a game regarded by most people as the best in the whole competition.

There had been some rain, which made the pitch nice and greasy, which favours the good players. Portugal had a team full of great players – Eusébio, Coluna, José Augusto, Simões and the giant centre forward, Torres. So we expected as difficult a match as it was possible to have, and that's how it turned out. But Alf, carefully and painstakingly had built a wonderful defensive system, and, long before the World Cup started, the back four of George Cohen, Jack Charlton, Bobby Moore and me, with Nobby Stiles just in front of us, had been a permanent fixture in the team, which shows what a splendid manager Alf Ramsey was. He built the team round a solid defence – only West Germany (twice) and Portugal scored against us – and that is the foundation of all successful sides.

Alf Ramsey was a super manager, a real thinker about the game. I don't think the general public realizes what he achieved. He was terrific.

Roger Hunt

Alf Ramsey was one of the all-time great managers, if not THE greatest. Every player liked him and respected him. He got on well with the players and always felt more at home with them than with officials or people from the media. The players always came first as far as he was concerned.

That was how Alf built the remarkable team spirit which existed in his day. Once you got into the side he regarded you as one of his players. Not just any old player, but HIS player, no matter which was your home club. In fact Alf regarded the English squad as a club.

He had a tremendous football brain. You have only to look at his record with Ipswich Town to see that. He took them from nothing to being the Champions in no time at all. And they did it by playing the sort of football everyone loves to see – or should love to see.

I'll tell you what. I'm proud to boast that I was one of Alf Ramsey's players.

Nobby Stiles

Sir Alf Ramsey? Now you're talking about one of the all-time greats. He was a brilliant manager. He took over an ordinary club, Ipswich Town, and in no time at all turned them into the No. 1 club in England. And he didn't spend a fortune doing it. No wonder the players were heartbroken when he left to become the England manager.

And with England he took over when we were down in the dumps. Three years later we were Champions of the World. The man was a raving genius. Ask any of the lads and they'll tell you the same.

He never seemed to write notes about anything. It was all in his head. I remember an incident just before the World Cup games began. We'd played Scotland, then gone on tour to Finland, Norway and Denmark and finished up in Poland. Then it was back to Lilleshall for the final training sessions before the big kick-off. While I was at Lilleshall wondering about the World Cup, my wife was at home having a baby! It didn't make me flavour of the month at home, but England came first.

Anyway, one day at Lilleshall, Alf started discussing the recent games we had played and he began with the one against Scotland. He turned to John Connelly and asked him how the third Scottish goal came about.

'I'm afraid I fouled one of their lads,' admitted John, 'and the big full back hoisted the free kick into our penalty area and Denis Law knocked it in.'

Alf nodded, and then, in that quiet, matter-of-fact voice of his, said, 'Yes, but there was a bit more to it than just that, wasn't there, John? When you committed the foul the ball went over the touchline and on to the track. You, Connelly, went to get the ball and you threw it to the big full back, so you were out of position when the free kick was taken. In future let them go and get the ball themselves. You just concentrate on taking up your right position.'

Frankly I had forgotten about the incident, but Alf refreshed my memory and left me speechless at his. But that was Alf. He had a great memory for detail. He didn't need videos to remind him what happened as the managers and coaches of today do. If the incident was worth remembering, Alf remembered it.

I remember when I had reason to be particularly grateful to him. I joined the England team in Gothenburg after playing for Manchester United in a European match, but I had mislaid the fluid I needed for my contact lenses. I told Alf and he dropped everything he was doing and set in motion the plan to fly in some.

He called Denis Follows, then Secretary of the Football Association, told him to find out the next flight out of London bound for Gothenburg and make certain that someone from the Football Association was at Heathrow to get the precious fluid on board. He gave Mr Follows the name of the fluid I needed.

When Alf was in full flight, giving his orders to all and sundry, an official asked him about some reception or other.

He was brushed aside as Alf told him the only matter of any importance to him at that moment was getting a supply of fluid so that I could wear my contact lenses. 'He can't play in glasses,' said Alf, 'so he needs contact lenses, and to wear contact lenses he needs this certain fluid. That is important, receptions and cocktail parties are not.'

I got the fluid.

Perhaps the most important thing Alf did was to instil in all of us a pride in playing for England. He believed that playing for your country was the greatest honour you could possibly win, and he was right. Anyone who would not be proud to pull on the England shirt would never play in Alf Ramsey's team.

It makes me laugh when I hear people say that Alf possessed none of life's nicest touches and that he had no sense of humour. They don't know that no matter what had happened in the match, whether we had won, lost or drawn, at breakfast the next morning Alf would go round to every table and thank each and every one of us playing for England. Yes, he thanked us for playing for England!

Jack Charlton

I know most of the lads swore by Alf – by him, not at him! But I had the feeling that he never really liked me and probably still doesn't. Maybe I was a bit too brash for him.

For instance, when I met him that Saturday night in the Hendon Hall Hotel and asked him why he had chosen me for England, he went on about Bobby Moore, who would always want to move up and play football on his way out of defence, and then he added, 'You see, Jack, I've picked you to cover for Bob's adventurous spirit. I pick the players I think will do the job I want them to do. They may not be the best players available, but they are the players who will do the job I give them.'

I said, 'Thanks, Alf' but I always had the feeling that I was one of those he regarded as 'not the best players'.

Well, maybe I wasn't, but I was still around in 1970 and went with the squad to Mexico. I didn't play in the quarter-final match against West Germany, when we lost 3–2 after leading 2–0. Brian Labone, of Everton, had taken my place.

Obviously, no one was very happy as we flew home and I thought a lot about my future. I realized that I'd come to the end of the road as far as international football was concerned, and I thought it might be a good idea to let Alf know how I felt.

There was an empty seat next to him a couple of rows behind me, so I went back and sat in the empty seat. The conversation was hilarious. I asked him if I could have a word with him, and he lowered the newspaper he was reading and said, 'What is it, Jack?' The dialogue was as follows:

ME: 'I've enjoyed playing for England, but I'm well into my thirties, so I think it would be wise if I called it a day.'
ALF: 'I totally agree.'

With that he lifted his newspaper and continued reading. Exit Jack Charlton from the international scene!

That might have been a bit of that impish humour some of the lads talked about.

Bobby Charlton

Alf produced a miracle with Ipswich. With England he did what few thought he could do – he won the World Cup, the only honour we have won.

What more can you say of the man?

12

The Players Look Back

Everybody in the country who was alive on that famous day in July 1966 has memories of the World Cup Final. Some were lucky enough to be at Wembley. Others had to make do with the television and radio coverage. But one thing is certain, nobody ignored the big game. People who did not usually follow soccer were interested. Even those who had no time for sport had time for the World Cup. The World Cup Final emptied the streets, cleared the beaches and kept a whole nation captive for at least two hours.

And what of the players, the twenty-two men who made up the World Cup squad? They, too, had their memories, and even the eleven who were not lucky enough to play in the Final were, nevertheless, proud to have been part of the winning squad.

For the record, the following eight players played in all six matches – Gordon Banks, George Cohen, Jack Charlton, Bobby Moore, Ray Wilson, Nobby Stiles, Bobby Charlton and Roger Hunt. Martin Peters played in five, Alan Ball, Jimmy Greaves and Geoff Hurst in three and the three recognized wingmen, Ian Callaghan, John Connelly and Terry Paine played in one each. Seven of the squad didn't play in any game. They were Peter Bonetti, Ron Springett, Jimmy Armfield, Gerry Byrne, Norman Hunter, Ron Flowers and George Eastham.

It speaks volumes for Alf Ramsey's management skills that eight players appeared in every match. Obviously his best team had been known to him for some time.

Sir Alf Ramsey is, and always has been, a modest man. When I asked him how proud he felt at having taken Ipswich Town from the old Third Division right up to the Championship of the old First Division, and following that by winning the World Cup, he replied, 'I didn't win the World Cup with England any more than I won the First Division Championship with Ipswich. The players won those honours. I just chose the right players.'

Having put the record straight on that, although few people would agree with him that his part was as minor as he suggests – after all, picking the right players isn't the easiest task in the world! – Sir Alf was happy to give his memories of the Final.

Alf Ramsey

The decision to choose an unchanged team for the World Cup Final was a difficult one, and I anguished over it for some time. But I was helped by the fact that I know the players were as anxious as I was that we should win the Cup, and they knew that I had an important job to do – that is, pick the team – and they knew that they had an important job to do – that is, go out there and win the Cup on the day.

It was tempting to risk Jimmy Greaves, despite his injury. He was England's leading goal scorer, he loved the big occasion and he was acknowledged throughout the world as a lethal finisher – one of the best there was anywhere.

But the team had performed magnificently in his absence. We had beaten two fancied teams in Argentina and Portugal, so I could not have asked for anything more. On top of that, Geoff Hurst, who had come into the side when Jimmy was injured, had done a great job. It was him or an injured Jimmy Greaves.

After a lot of thought, I decided to leave well alone. As they say, if a thing isn't broken, don't try to mend it. My decision turned out right, but I realize the amount of flak I would have had to take if we had lost. But that is the risk all managers have to take, and, anyway, we never talked about losing all the time we were together.

I felt sorry for Jim. He was a great player, he deserved to be a World Cup winner, but he was carrying an injury, he might not have lasted the full one hundred and twenty minutes and there were no substitutes in those days. On top of all that, Hurst was in magnificent form, as he showed in the Final. I had a clear conscience. I had to make a decision, and a decision that was best for the team and their chances of winning the World Cup.

Our victory didn't surprise me. I always knew we would win. I said so when I took the job as England manager, and I repeated my belief even after my first match in charge, which we lost 5–2.

All right, you can say that playing at Wembley was an advantage, but there was more to it than that. I had seen the squad settle into a real club, a club with the ability to win despite the fact that there were excellent sides around like Argentina, Portugal, West Germany and Russia.

The longer the Final lasted, the more confident I became that we were going to win. The spectators were wonderful with their support, but then so were the German supporters, and the main thing was that we were the better team on the day. My faith in the side was never shaken, even when the Germans scored the first goal. I still knew we would win.

When the final whistle went I was delighted. It was a victory for teamwork. We had worked together as one unit and everyone had done his job to the best of his ability. You cannot ask for more.

The victory in 1966 was a great moment. I was intensely proud of each and every one of the twenty-two members of the squad.

Ray Wilson

Once we had reached the Final I felt very confident that we would win the match. No disrespect to the Germans. They were a very good side, they had some excellent players, but I was convinced we were better than they were. I was fuming at my error which gave Germany their first goal, but there's only one way to get over an error like that: forget it and play better.

I don't think the Final was a great game if you were looking for classical football, but there were lots of controversial incidents which has kept people talking about the game more, perhaps, than any other World Cup Final. Once we had equalized their first goal in a short space of time, we were never in trouble, and at the end of ninety minutes they looked much more worried and tired than we were. We weren't worried, but we were tired, until, that is, Alf strolled up and told us that we didn't have time to be tired!

George Cohen

The most vivid memory of the World Cup Final is of tiredness. I'd had a long season with Fulham, playing in almost every game. On top of that, I'd had a spell in hospital and had to struggle to get fit again. It's not just the physical tiredness. It's a mental thing as well.

The physical tiredness evaporated during the short interval after ninety minutes with Alf saying, 'Come on, socks up, shirts tucked in, just think about what you are doing.' Somehow or other he injected energy into us and it showed in the one hundred and twentieth minute as Geoff raced away to score the fourth goal. I could see the defender with him, but whereas Geoff was going at a hell of a lick, the German was struggling. His legs had gone and that makes you move that little bit slower while the ball moves that little bit faster. A nasty combination!

As soon as the final whistle went, Nobby leapt at me, flung his arms around me and planted a huge kiss on me. It was so violent I felt I might be sucked into the gap in his teeth!

The whole feeling when I realized it was all over and we had won was one of sheer relief. It had been a hard grind but now it was over, the victory created elation which wiped away the tiredness. I looked at some of the Germans. They were as knackered as we were, perhaps even more than we were, and now they were faced with the depression of defeat. It couldn't have been easy for them.

I enjoyed the tournament, I enjoyed winning the tournament and when the truth of it all really sunk in I realized what a wonderful day it was. Let's face it, it was England's first triumph in the history of football.

That's why I was so disappointed in later years when I discovered how quickly the Football Association forgot. Twenty-fifth anniversaries are always celebrated in England, but the twenty-fifth anniversary of our World Cup win was practically ignored.

I understand that the only recognition of the twenty-fifth anniversary of our win was that some of the lads were

invited to Wembley for the FA Cup Final and were introduced to the crowd. The Football Association could and
should have done more. After all, if you can't take care of the
past you can't take care of the future. A great chance was
thrown away. We should have used the World Cup win to
instil more pride in our national side, to make the younger
players hungry to play for their country.

Jimmy Greaves

I was delighted for the lads. Everybody wanted England to
win, but nobody wanted England to win more than I did.
Nobody wanted to play in the Final more than I did, but I
knew it was impossible. I just wouldn't have lasted ninety
minutes, let alone one hundred and twenty.

I was gutted when I received the injury, and when it
became obvious that there was no way I could be one
hundred per cent by the Final day. I only wish I'd been
allowed to go home there and then. I could have gone along
to Tottenham each day for treatment, and I think that would
have been better than staying around with the team and feeling useless.

John Connelly

I had just the one game – against Uruguay – and I felt I did
pretty well. But Alf decided to give Terry Paine and Ian
Callaghan a game each so that he could decide which one of
us would suit him best. He decided that none of us suited
him and he was happy to have Alan Ball wide on the right
and Martin Peters looking after the left side. Who can say he
was wrong? We won didn't we?

Of course I was disappointed not to be in the side for the Final, but only eleven could play, and I can assure you that the most enthusiastic England supporters in the stadium that afternoon were us eleven who hadn't made it. We were all willing them to win from our seats in the stand, and then from the bench. We had moved there near to the end of extra-time thinking we had thoroughly deserved to win 2–1!

Little did we realize what was to come, but it all turned out for the best.

Ian Callaghan

I thought I would feel a sense of deep disappointment not being in the side for the Final. No footballer likes not being in the line-up, especially for such a big game, but eleven of us had to be disappointed, and results proved that Alf knew what he was doing.

Obviously, I wanted to be out there on the park, but it wasn't to be and I was just proud to have been part of the whole set-up. It was a fabulous experience. I had never had one like it, and I haven't had one like it since. Certainly, the next best thing to have played in the Final was to have been in the squad.

Ron Flowers

I was surprised to be chosen for the squad so I never expected to be in the final eleven. That meant that I wasn't all that disappointed at not getting a game. I must admit, though, that the atmosphere got to me on Final day. The eleven of us who were not in the line-up had excellent seats in the stand not far from the Royal Box and about five minutes from the end we were all escorted to the lift in the

Main Hall and we went down to what can only be called the Royal Tunnel. We then walked up the tunnel towards the bench so that we could be near the lads at the end of the match.

We were all happy because we were winning 2–1 but just as we emerged from the tunnel there was a great roar. I couldn't see the pitch at that time and I thought to myself, 'It's three one now.' Then I saw the Germans celebrating and my heart sank. But it all came right in the end.

We didn't watch the game like the ordinary spectators. Players watching rarely get very excited. We studied players carefully, watching for the good points and for the bad ones.

The man who impressed me most in the Final was Alan Ball. He ran everywhere. He was at his peak, wanting the ball all the time. I don't think I've ever seen him have a better game. He wanted the ball so much because he enjoyed running at Schnellinger and beating him. Schnellinger was a great full back with loads of experience, but Bally ran him ragged in the World Cup Final.

In the one hundred and twentieth minute, as Geoff Hurst was racing towards goal, Bally could see the defender with him, so he was screaming for a square pass from Geoff.

We could hear him quite clearly on the bench because he was on our side of the field. I saw Geoff look across to Bally, but there was no square pass: just a goal!

Geoff Hurst

Bobby Moore sent me an inch-perfect pass and I knew there were only seconds to go. The Germans had sent everyone forward to try and snatch an equalizer, so I was clear. I could see Bally steaming up over to my right and a square pass to him was on. I did glance over towards Alan and the guy chasing me must have noticed because he veered over to the right ever so slightly as if he was in two minds. So I had a shot, knowing that wherever the ball ended the game would be over. It went into the net.

Jimmy Armfield

We all wanted the lads to win, but we all wished we had been in the side. The spirit in the camp was terrific. We were really the back-up squad and we did all we could to boost morale.

Argentina was the team I feared. I respected Portugal, but somehow or other we always seemed to have the Indian sign on them, both at club and at international level.

Every World Cup winning side has at least one great star. In 1954 West Germany had Fritz Walter, in 1958, 1962 and in 1970 Brazil had Pelé, and in 1974 West Germany had Beckenbauer while Holland had Cruyff. In 1966 our ace in the pack was Bobby Charlton, and his two superb goals against Mexico set us on the right road.

Many people said that Alf kept his final selection a secret until the morning of the match. He might have done as far as the public and the media were concerned, but we all knew at least two days before. (In fact, we could all have guessed his team anyway.) The confirmation we had was when the eleven not needed played a game against Arsenal at London Colney. We won, and the lads carried me, the senior professional in the squad, off the pitch shoulder high.

My honest opinion is that if the eleven who played Arsenal in that friendly had played in the World Cup Final we would still have won. That's how good I think our strength in depth was.

You see, English football was at its strongest then because we were children of the war and as youngsters we had been deprived of a lot of what are called life's good things. In our football careers we had seen the bad times of the maximum wage and then tasted the benefits of the liberation from soccer slavery, which came in 1961.

That liberation began England's best period in world football. From 1961 until 1970 we were terrific – beaten by Brazil in the 1962 quarter-final, winners in 1966 and beaten by West Germany in the 1970 quarter-final. I don't think the general public realize how good we were.

At the Final, the eleven of us who were not playing showed all the signs of football superstition. I wore a red jumper to the Opening Ceremony and the game against Uruguay which followed, and I vowed I would wear it to every game until we were beaten. So the Final day was red jumper day for me … and I say I am not superstitious!

My room-mate was Norman Hunter. He was just as bad as me. He never went to watch the team play without carrying his mackintosh!

It had been agreed that near the end of the ninety minutes, no matter what the score was, I was to lead my ten colleagues down to ground level. We could then join Alf and the others on the bench.

We were a happy bunch as we went down. After all, we were winning 2–1. Then, as I emerged from the tunnel, I saw the German player take the free kick. Seconds later the ball was in the net. They'd equalized.

I don't think any of the other lads saw the ball go into the net.

Norman Hunter

I thought we were well on top in the second half, and as we followed Jim [Armfield] down to the bench I thought it was great. At least we'd be able to join in the celebrations. But the first thing I knew there was a great cheer and the Germans were celebrating. It was a bitter blow, but, I'm glad to say, not a fatal one.

Gordon Banks

By 30 July we were brimful of confidence. After the opening group games we'd had a tough run against Argentina and Portugal, both fine sides. Yet only Portugal had scored against us. They had a wonderful team. Coluna was great. There was little Simões on the wing, and the big fellow Torres in the middle heading the ball down to his colleagues. Then there was Eusébio. What can you say about him? A real genius.

I was mad when we conceded that first goal to the Germans, but a quick equalizer restored my confidence and, quite frankly, I couldn't see us losing. I thought Jack was unfairly penalized near the end, and from the free kick I had a clear view of Haller diverting the ball with his arm straight to Weber. I couldn't believe it when the referee gave a goal. But it all came right in the end, although I cannot understand why so much fuss has been made of our third goal when their second goal has been forgotten.

The journey from Wembley to the Royal Garden Hotel was unforgettable. The crowds lined the streets along the route and it was heart-warming to see them. Everyone was so happy and I thought to myself, 'Well, we've really done something this time.' There was chaos at the hotel because the coach couldn't get up the ramp to the front door so it was one hell of a struggle getting from the coach and into the hotel.

Alan Ball

It was the greatest day of my life. People say that I never stopped running. If I had stopped I don't think I would have been able to start again.

Even Nobby looked as if he'd had it at one time so I had to give him a right old rollicking in no uncertain terms. But we all seemed to get our second wind, and the sight of the Germans lying down in the short interval between the end of the ninety minutes and the start of extra-time gave us heart. It's worth remembering that if you give the opposition the slightest hint that you are tired you will give them a boost, and that's the last thing you want to do.

Gerry Byrne

I don't remember much about the Final. Those of us who were not playing all ran on to the pitch at the end and congratulated the lads.

I was envious of those who were chosen to play. I would have loved to have been out there, but there had to be eleven disappointed fellows who sat in the stand rather than played in the match.

It was a typical example of the camaraderie which existed among the squad that the players who played in the Final insisted that the £22,000 win bonus should be shared equally by all twenty-two members of the squad, but it was a disappointment that there were no medals for members of the squad. All right, there could only be eleven gold medals inscribed 'World Cup Winners', but it would have been nice to have been given a medal inscribed 'World Cup Winners 1966, Squad Member'.

It's surprising how consistent the football bosses are at spoiling the ship for a ha'porth of tar.

Roger Hunt

All anyone wants to know about the 1966 World Cup Final when they talk to me is, 'Was it a goal?' I don't want to fall back on the old cliché – 'Look at the record books' – but I can tell you this. Anyone who says the ball didn't cross the line after it hit the crossbar was not standing where I was. And where was I? No more than two yards from the goal-line. People who were no nearer the incident than behind the other goal have come out with their views, but I can tell you that after the ball hit the bar it swerved well over the goal-line. All those people who keep talking about whether all the ball was over the line when it landed are showing their ignorance of the laws. If the ball is over the line in mid-air, it's a goal, and I can tell you that Geoff Hurst's shot swerved well over the line after it struck the circular crossbar.

Nobby Stiles

An unforgettable day, wasn't it? We won, we won fairly, and the journey from the stadium to the hotel in the West End of London was something I'll never forget. I've never seen so many people, and it was wonderful to realize how much our victory had meant to the public.

Once we had fought our way into the Royal Garden Hotel we were told that we had to attend the official banquet with the players of the other three semi-finalists. Our wives had come down on the day before the match, but we didn't see them until we got to the hotel on the Saturday evening.

Then we heard the news. We were welcome at the banquet. All the officials and the guests were welcome, and so were their wives. But were ours? Not on your life. My wife had given birth to a baby while I had been at Lilleshall for the pre-World Cup training, and one accepts as part and parcel of the job that you can't break training. But to find out that you've won the World Cup and your wife wasn't welcome at the banquet sickened me. I was disgusted, and I still am.

Do you know what our wives were told? 'Don't worry, there's a meal laid on for you, and there's a television set in the room so you will be able to see your husbands on the box when the BBC come over.' Oh, big deal, thank you very much.

By about eleven o'clock I was fed up. So were most of the lads. I told Bobby Moore how we felt and that we wanted to leave, so he went to Alf and told him what we all wanted to do. Alf agreed, so we all left. Before we did so, Bobby Moore told us that we were all welcome at the Playboy Club in Park Lane.

I was the first to leave, along with Alan Ball, my roommate, and John Connelly. We picked up our wives and got a cab to the Playboy Club. When we arrived we were given a warm welcome and asked to stand in line. 'We want to take a picture of everyone here,' someone explained.

We weren't happy at having our pictures taken. You never know what people use them for. So we left and went along to Danny La Rue's club, where Danny and Ronnie Corbett were appearing in cabaret. We had a marvellous time there and really enjoyed our celebrations. They couldn't do enough for us at the club.

Geoff Hurst and his wife joined us later on, so, without a thought about how the official banquet was progressing, we just let our hair down and enjoyed ourselves.

But all good things have to come to an end, and as we prepared to leave we asked for the bill. The head waiter came up to us and said, 'Thank you, gentlemen, but Danny La Rue is picking up the tab. He's so proud of you, so proud of how you played, and so proud that you've come to his club.'

What a perfect gentleman.

Postscript

After the 1966 World Cup, relations between the BBC and myself began to sour. There were disputes about my status as No. 1 commentator, talk of new contracts, threats of injunctions … As early as February 1970, I was told I would not be covering the English matches.

With all this simmering in the background I went to Mexico for the 1970 World Cup and thoroughly enjoyed my time working with the late John McGonagle in Leon. When there were no matches we stayed in the Guadalajara Hilton with the rest of the BBC team and the England team.

The journey along crowded roads from Guadalajara to Leon was somewhat terrifying especially at night when the heavy lorries thundered along either so well lit that they were like travelling illuminations, or with no lights at all! During the day we were glad of our air-conditioned car with darkened windows, for the heat was stifling and the sunlight dazzling.

On the advice of our driver, we stopped at a town called Tepatitlan. We walked into a bar and ordered two gin and tonics. Nobody had heard of tonic water, so we promised to bring them a bottle on our next trip.

However, when we did, not a soul in the bar could drink the stuff!

Leon was a friendly city where the people loved to enjoy themselves. They had decorated their streets, and the local square was the scene each evening of great celebrations.

Facing the city square was the Hotel Condessa, where the Moroccan team were staying, and a livelier, more fun-loving bunch of characters you couldn't have wished to meet. They arrived in Mexico as real no-hopers. In fact their coach, Blagoje Vidinic, a former Yugoslav international goalkeeper whom I had seen play many times, admitted he could only find nineteen players good enough to make the trip, though each country was allowed a maximum of twenty-two. They were all amateurs, a mixture of Parachute Regiment officers, Army musicians, male nurses, farm workers and civil servants, but they almost produced the shock of the first round.

The no-hopers played West Germany, took the lead after only twenty minutes, held it for thirty-five minutes and were only beaten by a goal twelve minutes from the end.

Spending so many happy days in such delightful company made me put the main problem behind me. One day John McGonagle and I were asked by our driver if we would like to go to Tequila, which is not all that far from Guadalajara. We couldn't believe there was such a place, but there definitely is. We were taken round a tequila distillery and then each of us was presented with a special bottle of the famous Mexican drink. No, not ordinary tequila, but tequila that had been matured in oak casks for twelve years, and was, therefore, the colour of blended whisky.

We were told that each family owned a small plot of land and had planted a crop of the megay plant, from which tequila is distilled. The plant, which is a form of cactus, takes three years to grow, at which time the peasants sell the crop to the distillery, use some of the money to buy some more megay plants, which they sow in their plots of land, and the rest of the money is used to buy the odd tot of tequila and to finance them for the next three years ... until the next crop is ready.

And so a happy time in Mexico continued. It seemed that everywhere we went, guitarists popped up, put on their sombreros and serenaded us with *Guadalajara*.

Then the telephone call came. My solicitor rang to give me the worrying news about the BBC's intentions for the World Cup Final; in that week's *Radio Times* there was no mention of Kenneth Wolstenholme.

So, the very next day after the telephone call, which I must admit shattered me, even though I had half expected the news, I went to see Sam Leitch, who was one of the two Editors on the spot. I asked him outright whether I was doing the Final or not, and Sam replied that he didn't know: that decision would be taken in London.

Although because of the terms of my contract there shouldn't have been any doubt, I asked him to find out because we were now at the semi-final stage. Sam did and told me, 'Yes, you are doing the commentary on the Final and David [Coleman] is doing the scene set before the kick-off.'

But I couldn't help wondering whether the answer would have been the same if England had reached the Final.

What a Final we had in Mexico City. The 1970 Brazilian side is the best I have ever seen from that great footballing nation and it was a joy to watch them.

As if to celebrate Brazil's victory – or maybe join in the weeping for Italy's defeat – the heavens opened after the match in a deluge of alarming severity. But that didn't spoil the BBC party the same evening because we had just heard the wonderful news that Tony Jacklin had won the United States Open Golf Championship.

Nineteen sixty-six had been the beginning of the age of the summarizer. 1970 should have been the end of it. But by that time the craze had spread and was rampant throughout the game. Managers, players, former players were brought in to pon-tificate on the box and trot out their favourite clichés, such meaningless gems as 'they've got it all to do' or 'they'll be desperate to get a result'. Television commentators picked up such remarks and before you could say, 'They must keep it tight at the back,' you had a television newspeak long before the days of 'do I not like that'. Viewers were given tactical lessons, they had opinions thrust at them – and not all the comments were accurate.

In 1970 the BBC took Joe Mercer and Don Revie to Mexico as their on-the-spot men, but they were just the tip of the iceberg. Back home in England the studios were crowded with people only too willing to give their opinions, to analyse what they had seen and to argue about anything and everything. Sometimes they were left with egg on their faces.

All the pre-World Cup publicity about Mexico had been about the crippling altitude and the summarizers in London latched on to that, without realizing that Guadalajara, where England were based and where they played all their games except the quarter-final against West Germany, presented no altitude problems at all. Leon, where we met and lost to Germany was even less of a problem than Guadalajara.

A similar thing happened four years later when the finals were played in West Germany. I went to a game between

Scotland and Yugoslavia and it was so hot and humid that I could hardly breathe … and I was just watching.

Yet almost to a man, the summarizers in London heaped criticism upon both teams for their lethargy. None of them mentioned the stamina-sapping weather.

There are other reasons for mistrusting the remarks of someone who has watched the game in the comfort of a studio. The most important one is that television does not show the whole of the game. Even with the multiplicity of cameras used today it is impossible to show all the pitch, so the cameras follow the ball. That is fine for the entertainment of the viewers, but there are many important things which happen off the ball. Television can only show the culmination of the off-the-ball moves, which means that the viewers – AND the studio-based expert summarizers – can often miss the excellent build-up to a goal, or even a miss. The Hungarians in the 1950s researched their game so well that they discovered that even a star player is in possession of the ball for little, if any, more than four minutes of the ninety. When Joe Mercer was told of this he said, 'Which proves that it is vitally important what a player does for the other eighty-six.'

It is what that player is doing for the other eighty-six minutes that the television viewer cannot see. Nor can the studio-based experts.

The 1970 World Cup over, I entered the last year of my three-year contract with the BBC, and it was plain that the Corporation would find some way of watering down the terms of any renewal they might suggest. This they did at a meeting in April 1971. I was offered a new contract with a higher guarantee of income but without the all-important clause that I would cover all the major finals, FA Cup, World Cup etc.

This I refused to accept and Paul Fox confirmed that if

England had reached the 1970 Final in Mexico I would not have done the commentary. I didn't bother to tell him that I had a contingency plan to ensure that I would have done.

So it was the parting of the ways, but since my very last engagement for the BBC as a commentator – the 1971 European Cup Final between Ajax and Panathinaikos – I have been working hard and never been happier.

And never as happy as at the present, working on Italian football for Chrysalis Sport. Here is a young company, part of the Chrysalis Group plc, a company that doesn't have any prima donnas and a company that is deservedly going from strength to strength in the coverage of sport on television. Italian football is a wonderful product because Serie A produces the most skilful football of any league in the world. There are some who kid themselves that our Premiership does that, but as Alan Hansen so rightly said on television recently, 'The Premiership might be one of the most exciting leagues, but it is light years behind when it comes to skill.'

As I look back, it is remarkable that my words, 'They Think It's all over ... It is now' are as well known as ever. Sadly, they have been over used, one thing the BBC Sports Department tried to avoid.

However, once the Light Entertainment department used the words as the title for a comedy programme, the floodgates opened and the words have been used by all and sundry for various advertisements. When I asked John Birt what relation the words had to the television programme he told me he 'wanted to bring the famous words to the notice of the younger generation'.

I didn't bother to reply.

But not even the mis-use of my words, the brouhaha over getting the match ball back to Geoff Hurst, its rightful owner, or the thirty years which have elapsed since 1966 can dim the memory of England's greatest sporting triumph.

The 1966 World Cup Results

First Round

Group 1

ENGLAND	(0)	0	URUGUAY	(0)	0	Wembley – Att. 75,000
FRANCE	(0)	1	MEXICO	(0)	1	
Hausser			Borja			Wembley – Att. 55,000
URUGUAY	(2)	2	FRANCE	(1)	1	
Rocha, Cortes			de Bourgoing, pen.			White City – Att. 40,000
ENGLAND	(1)	2	MEXICO	(0)	0	
Charlton, R., Hunt						Wembley – Att. 85,000
MEXICO	(0)	0	URUGUAY	(0)	0	Wembley – Att. 35,000
ENGLAND	(1)	2	FRANCE	(0)	0	
Hunt (2)						Wembley – Att. 92,500

	P	W	D	L	For	Agnst	Pts
1. ENGLAND	3	2	1	0	4	0	5
2. URUGUAY	3	1	2	0	2	1	4
3. MEXICO	3	0	2	1	1	3	2
4. FRANCE	3	0	1	2	2	5	1

Qualified: Group Winners: ENGLAND
             Runners-up: URUGUAY

Group 2

WEST GERMANY	(3)	5	SWITZERLAND	(0)	0	
Held, Haller (2, 1 pen.),						
Beckenbauer (2)						Hillsborough – Att. 36,000
SPAIN	(0)	1	ARGENTINA	(0)	2	
Pirri			Artime (2)			Villa Park – Att. 42,738
SWITZERLAND	(1)	1	SPAIN	(0)	2	
Quentin			Sanchis, Amancio			Hillsborough – Att. 32,000
ARGENTINA	(0)	0	WEST GERMANY	(0)	0	Villa Park – Att. 46,587
ARGENTINA	(0)	2	SWITZERLAND	(0)	0	
Artime, Onega						Hillsborough – Att. 32,127
SPAIN	(1)	1	WEST GERMANY	(1)	2	
Fuste			Emmerich, Seeler			Villa Park – Att. 45,187

	P	W	D	L	For	Agnst	Pts
1. WEST GERMANY	3	2	1	0	7	1	5
2. ARGENTINA	3	2	1	0	4	1	5
3. SPAIN	3	1	0	2	4	5	2
4. SWITZERLAND	3	0	0	3	1	9	0

Qualified: Group Winners: WEST GERMANY
             Runners-up: ARGENTINA

Group 3

BULGARIA	(0)	0	BRAZIL Pelé, Garrincha	(1)	2	Goodison Park – Att. 47,308
HUNGARY Bene	(0)	1	PORTUGAL José Augusto (2) Torres	(1)	3	Old Trafford – Att. 29,886
BRAZIL Tostao	(1)	1	HUNGARY Bene, Farkas, Meszöly, pen.	(1)	3	Goodison Park – Att. 51,387
PORTUGAL Vutzov own goal, Eusébio, Torres	(2)	3	BULGARIA	(0)	0	Old Trafford – Att. 25,438
PORTUGAL Simoes, Eusébio (2)	(2)	3	BRAZIL Rildo	(0)	1	Goodison Park – Att. 58,479
HUNGARY Davidov own goal, Meszöly, Bene	(2)	3	BULGARIA Asparukhov	(1)	1	Old Trafford – Att. 24,129

	P	W	D	L	For	Agnst	Pts
1. PORTUGAL	3	3	0	0	9	2	6
2. HUNGARY	3	2	0	1	7	5	4
3. BRAZIL	3	1	0	2	4	6	2
4. BULGARIA	3	0	0	3	1	8	0

Qualified: Group Winners: PORTUGAL
Runners-up: HUNGARY

Group 4

RUSSIA Malofeev (2), Banishevsky	(2)	3	NORTH KOREA	(0)	0	Ayresome Park – Att. 23,006
CHILE	(0)	0	ITALY Mazzola, Barison	(1)	2	Roker Park – Att. 27,199
NORTH KOREA Pak Seung Zin	(0)	1	CHILE Marcos, pen.	(1)	1	Ayresome Park – Att. 13,792
ITALY	(0)	0	RUSSIA Chislenko	(0)	1	Roker Park – Att. 27,793
ITALY	(0)	0	NORTH KOREA Pak Doo lk	(0)	1	Ayresome Park – Att. 17,829
CHILE Marcos	(1)	1	RUSSIA Porkujan (2)	(1)	2	Roker Park – Att. 16,027

	P	W	D	L	For	Agnst	Pts
1. RUSSIA	3	3	0	0	6	1	6
2. NORTH KOREA	3	1	1	1	2	4	3
3. ITALY	3	1	0	2	2	2	2
4. CHILE	3	0	1	2	2	5	1

Qualified: Group Winners: RUSSIA
Runners-up: NORTH KOREA

The Quarter Finals

ENGLAND	(0)	1	ARGENTINA	(0)	0	
Hurst						Wembley – Att. 88,000
RUSSIA	(1)	2	HUNGARY	(0)	1	
Chislenko, Porkujan			Bene			Roker Park – Att. 22,103
PORTUGAL	(2)	5	NORTH KOREA	(3)	3	
Eusébio 4 (2 pens.),			Pak Seung Zin,			
José Augusto			Li Dong Woon,			
			Yang Sung Kook			Goodison Park – Att. 42,248
WEST GERMANY	(1)	4	URUGUAY	(0)	0	
Held, Beckenbauer,						
Seeler, Haller						Hillsborough – Att. 40,007

The Semi Finals

WEST GERMANY	(1)	2	RUSSIA	(0)	1	
Haller, Beckenbauer			Porkujan			Goodison Park – Att. 38,273
ENGLAND	(1)	2	PORTUGAL	(0)	1	
R. Charlton (2)			Eusébio, pen.			Wembley – Att. 90,000

Match for the 3rd and 4th Places

PORTUGAL	(1)	2	RUSSIA	(1)	1	
Eusébio, pen., Torres			Malofeev			Wembley – Att. 70,000

World Cup Final

ENGLAND	(1)	4	WEST GERMANY	(1)	2	
Hurst (3), Peters			Haller, Weber			Wembley – Att. 93,000

After extra time – 90 mins, 2–2

Final Placings

1. ENGLAND
2. WEST GERMANY
3. PORTUGAL
4. RUSSIA

All the Teams, Scores and Scorers

Monday 11 July

Group 1 at Wembley: ENGLAND 0, URUGUAY 0
ENGLAND: Banks; Cohen, Jack Charlton, Moore, Wilson; Stiles,
  Bobby Charlton, Ball; Greaves, Hunt, Connelly.
URUGUAY: Mazurkieviez; Troche; Ubiñas, Manicera, Gonçalvez,
  Caetano; Viera, Cortes, Rocha; Silva, Perez.
Referee: Istvan Zsolt of Hungary.

Tuesday 12 July

Group 2 at Hillsborough: WEST GERMANY 5, SWITZERLAND, 0
WEST GERMANY: Tilkowski; Hottges, Schulz, Weber, Schnellinger;
  Beckenbauer, Overath; Bruells, Haller, Seeler, Held.
SWITZERLAND: Elsener; Grobéty, Schneiter, Tacchella, Fuhrer; Bäni,
  Dürr; Odermatt, Künzli, Hosp, Schindelholz.
Referee: Hugh Phillips of Scotland.
Scorers: HELD, HALLER (2, 1 penalty), BECKENBAUER (2) (for West
  Germany).

Group 3 at Goodison Park: BRAZIL 2, BULGARIA 0
BRAZIL: Gylmar; Djalma Santos, Bellini, Altair, Henrique; Denilson,
  Lima; Garrincha, Alcindo, Pelé, Jairzinho.
BULGARIA: Naidenov; Shalamanov, Penev, Vutzov, Gaganelov;
  Kitov, Zhechev, Yakimov; Dermendjiev, Asparukhov, Kolev.
Referee: Kurt Tschenscher of West Germany.
Scorers: PÉLE, GARRINCHA (for Brazil).

Group 4 at Ayresome Park: RUSSIA 3, NORTH KOREA 0
RUSSIA: Kavazashvili; Ponomarev, Khurtsilava, Ostrovsky,
  Shesternev; Sabo, Sichinava; Chislenko, Banishevsky, Malofeev,
  Khusainov.
NORTH KOREA: Li Chan Myung; Pak Li Sup, Kang Bong Chil, Lim
  Zoong Sun, Shin Yung Kyoo; Im Seung Hwi, Pak Doo Ik; Pak
  Seung Zin, Kang Ryong Woon, Han Bong Zin, Kim Seung Il.
Referee: Juan Gardeazabal of Spain.
Scorers: MALOFEEV (2), BANISHEVSKY (for Russia).

Wednesday 13 July

Group 1 at Wembley: FRANCE 1, MEXICO 1
FRANCE: Aubour; Djorkaeff, Artelesa, Budzynski, de Michele; Bosquier, Bonnel, Herbin; Combin, Gondet, Hausser.
MEXICO: Calderón; Chaires, Peña, Nuñez, Hernández; Diáz, Mercado; Reyes, Borja, Fragoso, Padilla.
Referee: Menachem Askeas of Israel.
Scorers: HAUSSER (for France), BORJA (for Mexico).

Group 2 at Villa Park: ARGENTINA 2, SPAIN 1
ARGENTINA: Roma; Perfumo, Marzolini, Ferreiro, Albrecht; Solari, Rattin, Gonzalez; Artime, Onega, Mas.
SPAIN: Iribar; Sanchis, Pirri, Gallego, Eladio; Del Sol, Zoco, Suarez; Ufarte, Peiró, Gento.
Referee: Dimiter Roumentchev of Bulgaria.
Scorers: ARTIME (2) (for Argentina), PIRRI (for Spain).

Group 3 at Old Trafford: PORTUGAL 3, HUNGARY 1
PORTUGAL: Carvalho; Morais, Baptista; Vicente, Hilário; Graca, Coluna; José Augusto, Eusébio, Torres, Simoes.
HUNGARY: Szentmihályi; Mátrai; Káposzta, Meszöly, Sipos, Sóvari; István Nagy; Farkas; Bene, Albert, Rákosi.
Referee: Leo Callaghan of Wales.
Scorers: JOSÉ AUGUSTO (2), TORRES (for Portugal), BENE (for Hungary).

Group 4 at Roker Park: ITALY 2, CHILE 0
ITALY: Albertosi; Burgnich, Rosato, Salvadore, Facchetti; Lodetti, Rivera, Perani; Bulgarelli, Mazzola, Barison.
CHILE: Olivares; Eyzaguirre, Figueroa, Cruz, Villanueva; Prieto, Marcos; Araya, Tobar, Fouilloux, Sanchez.
Referee: Gottfried Dienst of Switzerland.
Scorers: MAZZOLA, BARISON (for Italy).

Friday 15 July

Group 1 at White City: URUGUAY 2, FRANCE 1
URUGUAY: Mazurkieviez; Troche; Ubiñas, Gonçalvez, Manicera,
  Caetano; Viera, Cortes, Rocha; Sacia, Perez.
FRANCE: Aubour; Djorkaeff, Artelesa, Budzynski, Bosquier; Bonnel,
  Simon, Herbet; Gondet, de Bourgoing, Hausser.
Referee: Dr. Karol Galba of Czechoslovakia.
Scorers: ROCHA, CORTES (for Uruguay) DE BOURGOING penalty
  (for France).

Group 2 at Hillsborough: SPAIN 2, SWITZERLAND 1
SPAIN: Iribar; Sanchis, Pirri, Gallego, Reija; Zoco, Del Sol, Suarez;
  Amancio, Peiró, Gento.
SWITZERLAND: Elsener; Brodmann, Fuhrer, Leimgruber, Stierli;
  Armbruster, Bäni, Kuhn; Gottardi, Hosp, Quentin.
Referee: Tofik Bakhramov of Russia.
Scorers: SANCHIS, AMANCIO (for Spain), QUENTIN (for
  Switzerland).

Group 3 at Goodison Park: HUNGARY 3, BRAZIL 1
HUNGARY: Gelei; Mátrai; Káposzta, Meszöly, Sipos, Szepesi;
  Mathesz, Farkas; Bene, Albert, Rákosi.
BRAZIL: Gylmar; Djalma Santos, Bellini, Altair, Henrique; Gerson,
  Lima; Garrincha, Alcindo, Tostao, Jairzinho.
Referee: Ken Dagnall of England
Scorers: BENE, FARKAS, MESZÖLY penalty (for Hungary), TOSTAO
  (for Brazil).

Group 4 at Ayresome Park: NORTH KOREA 1, CHILE 1
NORTH KOREA: Li Chan Myung; Pak Li Sup, Shin Yung Kyoo, Lim
  Zoong Sun, Oh Yoon Kyung; Im Seung Hwi, Pak Seung Zin; Pak
  Doo Ik; Han Bong Zin, Kim Seung Il, Li Dong Woon.
CHILE: Olivares; Valentini, Cruz, Figueroa, Villanueva; Marcos,
  Prieto; Fouilloux, Landa, Araya, Sanchez.
Referee: Aly Kandil of the United Arab Republic.
Scorers: PAK SEUNG ZIN (for North Korea), MARCOS penalty (for
  Chile).

Saturday 16 July

Group 1 at Wembley: ENGLAND 2, MEXICO 0
ENGLAND: Banks; Cohen, Jack Charlton, Moore, Wilson; Stiles,
   Bobby Charlton, Peters; Paine, Greaves, Hunt.
MEXICO: Calderón; Del Muro; Chaires, Peña, Nuñez, Hernández;
   Juaregui, Diáz, Reyes, Borja, Padilla.
Referee: Concetto Lo Bello of Italy.
Scorers: BOBBY CHARTON, HUNT (for England).

Group 2 at Villa Park: ARGENTINA 0, WEST GERMANY 0
ARGENTINA: Roma; Perfumo, Ferreiro, Albrecht, Marzolini; Solari,
   Rattin, Gonzalez; Artime, Onega, Mas.
WEST GERMANY: Tilkowski; Hottges, Schulz, Weber, Schnellinger;
   Haller, Beckenbauer, Overath; Bruells, Seeler, Held.
Referee: Konstantin Zecevic of Yugoslavia.

Group 3 at Old Trafford: PORTUGAL 3, BULGARIA 0
PORTUGAL: Pereira; Festa, Germano, Vicente, Hilário; Graca,
   Coluna; José Augusto, Torres, Eusébio, Simoes.
BULGARIA: Naidenov; Shalamanov, Penev, Vutzov, Gaganelov;
   Zhechev, Yakimov; Dermendjiev, Zhekov, Asparukhov, Kostov.
Referee: Jose Maria Codesal of Uruguay.
Scorers: VUTZOV own goal, EUSÉBIO, TORRES (for Portugal).

Group 4 at Roker Park: RUSSIA 1, ITALY 0
RUSSIA: Yashin; Ponomarev, Shesternev, Khurtsilava, Danilov; Sabo,
   Voronin; Chislenko, Malofeev, Banishevsky, Khusainov.
ITALY: Albertosi; Burgnich, Rosato, Salvadore, Facchetti; Bulgarelli,
   Lodetti, Leoncini; Meroni, Mazzola, Pascutti.
Referee: Rudolf Kreitlein of West Germany.
Scorers: CHISLENKO (for Russia)

Tuesday 19 July

Group 1 at Wembley: MEXICO 0, URUGUAY 0
MEXICO: Carbajal; Chaires, Peña, Nuñez, Hernández; Diáz, Reyes,
    Mercado; Borja, Cisneros, Padilla.
URUGUAY: Mazurkieviez; Troche; Ubiñas, Manicera, Gonçalvez,
    Caetano; Cortes, Viera, Rocha; Sacia, Perez.
Referee: Bertil Loow of Sweden.

Group 2 at Hillsborough: ARGENTINA 2, SWITZERLAND 0
ARGENTINA: Roma; Perfumo, Calics, Ferreiro, Marzolini; Gonzalez,
    Solari, Rattin; Onega, Artime, Mas.
SWITZERLAND: Eichmann; Fuhrer, Brodmann, Stierli, Armbruster;
    Bäni, Kuhn; Gottardi, Hosp, Künzli, Quentin.
Referee: Joaquim Fernandes Campos, of Portugal.
Scorers: ARTIME, ONEGA (for Argentina).

Group 3 at Goodison Park: PORTUGAL 3, BRAZIL 1
PORTUGAL: Pereira; Morais, Baptista, Vicente, Hilário; Graca,
    Coluna; José Augusto, Eusébio, Torres, Simoes.
BRAZIL: Manga; Fidelis, Brito, Orlando, Rildo; Denilson, Lima;
    Jairzinho, Silva, Pelé, Parana.
Referee: George McCabe of England.
Scorers: SIMOES, EUSÉBIO (2) (for Portugal), RILDO (for Brazil).

Group 4 at Ayresome Park: NORTH KOREA 1, ITALY 0
NORTH KOREA: Li Chan Myung; Lim Zoong Sun, Shin Yung Kyoo,
    Ha Jung Won, Oh Yoon Kyung; Im Seung Hwi, Pak Seung Zin;
    Han Bong Zin, Pak Doo Ik, Kim Bong Hwan, Yang Sung Kook.
ITALY: Albertosi; Landini, Janich, Guarneri, Facchetti; Bulgarelli,
    Fogli, Perani; Mazzola, Rivera, Barison.
Referee: Pierre Schwinte of France.
Scorers: PAK DOO IK (for North Korea).

Wednesday 20 July

Group 1 at Wembley: ENGLAND 2, FRANCE 0
ENGLAND: Banks; Cohen, Jack Charlton, Moore, Wilson; Stiles,
  Bobby Charlton, Peters; Callaghan, Greaves, Hunt.
FRANCE: Aubour; Djorkaeff, Artelesa, Budzynski, Bosquier; Bonnel,
  Herbin, Simon; Herbet, Gondet, Hausser.
Referee: Arturo Yamasaki of Peru.
Scorers: HUNT (2) (for England).

Group 2 at Villa Park: WEST GERMANY 2, SPAIN 1
WEST GERMANY: Tilkowski; Hottges, Schulz, Weber, Schnellinger;
  Beckenbauer, Overath; Kraemer, Seeler, Held, Emmerich.
SPAIN: Iribar; Sanchis, Reija, Glaría, Gallego; Zoco, Pirri, Fusté;
  Amancio, Marcelino, Lapetra.
Referee: Armando Marques of Brazil.
Scorers: EMMERICH, SEELER (for West Germany), FUSTÉ (for
  Spain).

Group 3 at Old Trafford: HUNGARY 3, BULGARIA 1
HUNGARY: Gelei; Mátrai; Káposzta, Meszöly, Sipos, Szepesi;
  Mathesz, Farkas; Bene, Albert, Rákosi.
BULGARIA: Simeonov; Penev, Largov, Vutzov, Gaganelov; Zhechev,
  Davidov, Zhekov; Asparukhov, Kotkov, Kolev.
Referee: Roberto Goicoechea of Argentina.
Scorers: DAVIDOV own goal, MESZÖLY, BENE (for Hungary),
  ASPARUKHOV (for Bulgaria).

Group 4 at Roker Park: RUSSIA 2, CHILE 1
RUSSIA: Kavazashvili; Getmanov, Shesternev, Korneev, Ostrovsky,
  Afonin, Voronin, Serebrjannikov; Metreveli, Markarov, Porkujan.
CHILE: Olivares; Valentini, Cruz, Figueroa, Villanueva; Marcos,
  Prieto; Araya, Landa, Yavar, Sanchez.
Referee: John Adair of Northern Ireland.
Scorers: PORKUJAN (2) (for Russia), MARCOS (for Chile).

The Quarter Finals

Saturday 23 July

At Wembley: ENGLAND 1, ARGENTINA 0
ENGLAND: Banks; Cohen, Jack Charlton, Moore, Wilson; Stiles,
  Bobby Charlton, Peters; Ball, Hunt, Hurst.
ARGENTINA: Roma; Ferreiro, Perfumo, Albrecht, Marzolini;
  Gonzalez, Rattin, Solari, Onega; Artime, Mas.
Referee: Rudolf Kreitlein of West Germany.
Scorers: HURST (for England).

At Hillsborough: WEST GERMANY 4, URUGUAY 0
WEST GERMANY: Tilkowski; Hottges, Schulz, Weber, Schnellinger;
  Beckenbauer, Overath; Haller, Seeler, Held, Emmerich.
URUGUAY: Mazurkieviez; Troche; Ubiñas, Manicera, Gonçalvez,
  Caetano; Rocha, Salva, Cortes, Silva, Perez.
Referee: Jim Finney of England.
Scorers: HELD, BECKENBAUER, SEELER, HALLER (for West
  Germany).

At Goodison Park: PORTUGAL 5, NORTH KOREA 3
PORTUGAL: Pereira; Morais, Baptista, Vicente, Hilário; Graca,
  Coluna; José Augusto, Eusébio, Torres, Simoes.
NORTH KOREA: Li Chan Myung; Lim Zoong Sun, Shin Yung Kyoo,
  Ha Jung Won, Oh Yoon Kyung; Pak Seung Zin; Im Seung Hwi,
  Han Bong Zin, Pak Doo Ik, Li Dong Woon, Yang Sung Kook.
Referee: Menachem Ashkenasi of Israel.
Scorers: EUSÉBIO (4, 2 penalties), JOSÉ AUGUSTO (for Portugal),
  PAK SEUNG ZIN, LI DONG WOON, YANG SUNG KOOK (for
  North Korea).

At Roker Park: RUSSIA 2, HUNGARY 1
RUSSIA: Yashin; Ponomarev, Shesternev, Voronin, Danilov; Sabo,
  Khusainov; Chislenko, Banishevsky, Malofeev, Porkujan.
HUNGARY: Gelei; Mátrai; Káposzta, Sipos, Meszöly, Szepesi; István
  Nagy, Farkas; Bene, Albert, Rákosi.
Referee: Juan Gardeazabal of Spain.
Scorers: CHISLENKO, PORKUJAN (for Russia), BENE (for Hungary).

The Semi-Finals

Monday 25 July

At Goodison Park: WEST GERMANY 2, RUSSIA 1
WEST GERMANY: Tilkowski; Lutz, Schulz, Weber, Schnellinger;
    Beckenbauer, Haller, Overath; Seeler, Held, Emmerich.
RUSSIA: Yashin; Ponomarev, Shesternev, Voronin, Danilov; Sabo,
    Khusainov; Chislenko, Banishevsky, Malofeev, Porkujan.
Referee: Concetto Lo Bello of Italy.
Scorers: HALLER, BECKENBAUER (for West Germany), PORKUJAN
    (for Russia).

Tuesday 26 July

At Wembley: ENGLAND 2, PORTUGAL 1
ENGLAND: Banks; Cohen, Jack Charlton, Moore, Wilson; Stiles,
    Bobby Charlton, Peters; Ball, Hurst, Hunt.
PORTUGAL: Pereira; Festa, Baptista, José Carlos, Hilário; Graca,
    Coluna; José Augusto, Eusébio, Torres, Simoes.
Referee: Pierre Schwinte of France.
Scorers: BOBBY CHARLTON (2) (for England), EUSÉBIO penalty (for
    Portugal).

Match for 3rd and 4th Places

Thursday 28 July

At Wembley: PORTUGAL 2, RUSSIA 1
PORTUGAL: Pereira; Festa, Baptista, José Carlos, Hilário; Graca,
    Coluna; José Augusto, Eusébio, Torres, Simoes.
RUSSIA: Yashin; Ponomarev, Khurtsilava, Korneev, Danilov; Voronin,
    Sichinava, Serebrjannikov; Metreveli, Malofeev, Banishevsky.
Referee: Kenneth Dagnall of England.
Scorers: EUSÉBIO penalty, TORRES (for Portugal), MALOFEEV (for
    Russia).

The Final

Saturday 30 July 1966

At Wembley: ENGLAND 4, WEST GERMANY 2
   (after extra time)
ENGLAND: Banks; Cohen, Jack Charlton, Moore, Wilson; Stiles,
   Bobby Charlton, Peters; Ball, Hurst, Hunt.
WEST GERMANY: Tilkowski; Hottges, Schulz, Weber, Schnellinger;
   Beckenbauer, Haller, Overath; Seeler, Held, Emmerich.
Referee: Gottfried Dienst of Switzerland.
Scorers: HURST (3), PETERS (for England), HALLER, WEBER (for
   West Germany).